GW00400229

Susan is a Medium & Clairvoyant and has had communication with the spirit world since being a baby. She conducts private readings from home & by telephone for people all over the world.

Both Worlds-Living everyday with the dead is the first book based on Susan's life, which was put into book form with the help of her sister Barbara Grant. She has already started work on her second book. She lives at home in Hertfordshire with her husband and their two dogs.

BOTH WORLDS

Living everyday with the dead

Susan Bond

with Barbara Grant

BOTH WORLDS
Living everyday with the dead

Vanguard Press

VANGUARD PAPERBACK

© Copyright 2011
Susan Bond with Barbara Grant

The right of Susan Bond with Barbara Grant to be identified as authors
of this work has been asserted by them in accordance with the
Copyright, Designs and Patents Act 1988.

All Rights Reserved

No reproduction, copy or transmission of this publication
may be made without written permission.
No paragraph of this publication may be reproduced,
copied or transmitted save with the written permission of the publisher,
or in accordance with the provisions
of the Copyright Act 1956 (as amended).

Any person who commits any unauthorised act in relation to
this publication may be liable to criminal prosecution and
civil claims for damages.

All names have been changed for the privacy of the family.

A CIP catalogue record for this title is
available from the British Library.

ISBN 978 1 84386 920 7

*Vanguard Press is an imprint of
Pegasus Elliot MacKenzie Publishers Ltd.*
www.pegasuspublishers.com

First Published in 2011

**Vanguard Press
Sheraton House Castle Park
Cambridge England**

Printed & Bound in Great Britain

Disclaimer

All names have been changed for the privacy of the family.

Acknowledgements

After eleven years of drafting this book, it has at last been completed and published.

I would like to thank my sister Barbara Grant for helping me put these writings into book form – you have been very supportive in not only this process, but in all areas of my life.

I would like to thank my children and grandchildren for their support and more importantly their love.

Thanks to my husband for his patience for helping me with my ignorance of new technology (!) and his constant support.

Thank you to my dear friend Leslie Cornish – you are a true friend and talented medium.

I would like to thank everyone at Pegasus Elliot Mackenzie Publishers Ltd.

And most of all, my deepest gratitude and love to Michael, my spirit guide. You continually inspire and guide me through my life.

In dedication to my mum and dad, I forgive you.

CHAPTER 1

A Beginning

Summer 1959, it was one of those days where the air carries a threat of the storm to come. The Lennox children, four-year-old Eve and two-year-old Joe, sat in the back of a two-tone Austin Cambridge A55 with Mum and Dad in the front, on the road to Clacton. It was only for a day out, God knows there were precious few of them, but they never arrived.

Many years later Eve recalls the oppressive heat that made her clothes sticky. All the windows in the borrowed car were open, but the air remained stagnant. Dad was making the most of this rare trip, trying his best to keep things upbeat. Mum sat staring straight ahead, seemingly oblivious to his light-hearted chatter, absorbed in her own deep concerns. With hindsight Eve believes the trip was Dad's attempt to cheer up the family and provide a distraction for Mum from the dark news she was coping with.

Suddenly a cloud of black 'thunderbugs' also known as 'stormbugs' or 'thrips' (small flying insects that resemble black lines) filled the car, like an awful choking smoke, hampering Dad's already questionable driving skills. He swerved off the quiet country road, and the Austin ended up stuck in a roadside ditch at a sharp forty-five degree angle.

Eve remembers screaming and getting a mouth full of bugs for her trouble. Meanwhile Joe was sobbing uncontrollably and Mum was plain hysterical. Dad was quiet for what seemed like an eternity, but eventually started swearing, "Ruddy Hell, Ruddy, Ruddy Hell!" This was the absolutely worse thing that ever came out of his mouth in his whole lifetime, and only added to the sense of fear Eve and Joe already felt.

The position they were in meant it was extremely difficult to climb out of the motor, and the panic they all felt (except Dad), with the shock of the accident and about the bugs, meant that they were in no fit state to clamber out anyway. How long was it? Three minutes, thirty? Eventually an old couple approached the car and pulled them out. Eve remembers the lady smelt of old lavender, just like all old ladies smelt in 1959, and the man seemed well-to-do but still wore a tweedy working man's style cap.

The old couple took them all back to their bungalow, only one of two, set slightly back along this stretch of quiet country road. Eve cannot remember how the couple alerted the emergency services, which by today's standards was a complete joke as they took forever to respond, but she remembers the state Mum was in when they arrived.

"God help me!" she was shouting, "I've got his rotting dead baby inside me, and now this!" Eve recalls Mum's tears and sweaty face as she screamed at the ambulance man, "For God's sake what have I done to deserve this!"

"Come on Vi, calm down," Dad tried to reassure her. "We are all ok, just a few bumps and bruises, it could have been a lot worse."

"You hateful pig! You have no idea do you!" she spat at him. The whole room went quiet and Dad began shaking. The hurt in his eyes was visible, and he only just managed to stop the tears in his eyes from rolling down his face before turning his back on Eve and Joe, so as not to upset them further.

The ambulance man asked Mum to rest back on the settee whilst he checked her abdomen. She called him a silly man saying, "The top doctors have told me it's dead, I am due to have it surgically removed on Monday, you are being ridiculous."

"Please Mrs Lennox," he said, "I have to check." He began to examine her 'bump' and listened for a heartbeat. Eve says he looked 'funny' and went very white. He said to Mum, "Your baby is alive, I can hear a heartbeat and I felt it move."

Mum began to laugh hysterically; she was beside herself with what was essentially a cruel, cruel grief and some inexperienced ambulance man telling her the opposite of what the top obstetrician had said. She was probably on the verge of a breakdown that day – and Eve said it was the strangest most terrifying laugh she had ever heard, before or since.

Dad said, "Come on mate, don't make things worse, she's already on the edge, get her to hospital or something."

"Mr Lennox I assure you the baby is alive and kicking," as he finished saying this Mum's 'bump' did move and an unmistakable foot pushed up under her flesh.

Dad shouted, "My God, it's a miracle!" The old couple, who had both stood quietly in the corner of their living room all this while, were clapping their hands and smiling broadly.

Eve then remembers the ambulance men wanted to take Mum to hospital for further checks, but she pleaded with Dad not to go, she just wanted to get back to Slough to see what the specialist said.

Somehow we all got home – the car Dad had borrowed from Mum's brother, Uncle Tom, was a 'write-off' and Uncle Tom never came to see us much after that.

Although Mum had had two births at home prior to my endeavour to be a viable life, the obstetrician advised Mum to have me in the hospital. He said she 'was a special case', what he meant was he had made a mistake by saying your kid is dead, and, although litigation was not what it is today, he thought it best for his reputation, and possibly his pocket, that nothing else went wrong. Medical opinion was that I would be unlikely to be born alive in any case.

Apparently one of the junior doctors, in the middle of his training and on his 'Maternity' stint, saw Mum at the beginning of her labour. He made so bold as to guess the baby would be less than 5lb (in those days this was a rather low weight), and that if it was any more than that he would buy it a bonnet.

July 31st 1959 at 23.35 hours I was born – alive!

Weight 5lb 2ozs – pink bonnet from junior doctor – relieved obstetrician.

Whereas Dad and I have a special bond, one that has lasted his whole life and beyond, Mum and I never 'connected'. Although I believe I tried on many occasions to be the child (and adult) she wanted, she wasn't interested in me in the slightest. There was no pleasing her as far as I was concerned, no matter what I did or what I said it would always be wrong. How can a child even begin to understand how to tackle the emotional mind games that adults play, or even comprehend that they are playing them? Maybe she was jealous; maybe I was just 'in the way'. Obviously it must have been hard for her thinking I was dead inside her – perhaps almost coming to terms with that, then being told I was still alive but there could be problems at birth. Perhaps she just would not 'hope' too much in case I did not make it, and then when I did she wasn't ready to love me. Dad called me his 'Little Miracle' and he loved me so much. Dad loved all his kids, but his faith in the Catholic Church and the Lord God Almighty being what it was, meant he truly believed in the possibility of miracles.

I knew Mum never liked me; I only hoped that, at least, she didn't despise me. For the most part – once I understood what I could and could not speak about – I tried to keep my head down and get on with it. But when Dad called me his 'Little Miracle' it always seemed to upset Mum and she would look at me as though she hated me, or, even worse than that, with an air of indifference that I could hardly bear – Oh Mum…

One of my earliest memories is of lying in my pram looking up at the smiling faces of friends and relations who came to talk to me. I especially remember my Nan, Dad's mum, who came to see me every day without fail. It was much later that I realised she had died in 1957, two years before I was born. She would coo softly at me and make me feel safe; I felt such love from her that she made everything alright. Some days she took me out of the pram and cuddled and caressed me. Mum left me huddled up in a blanket in the hallway (out of the way) all day every day. Nan often took me out of the pram and whirled me round in the front room, secure in her arms, so I could see what was happening, and then plant a massive kiss on my forehead before tucking me back up in my pram. I grew to love her very deeply too; I often thought, 'Well, if Mum don't love me at least Nan and Dad do!' It still hurt though. What I could not have known at the time was that the man with the kind and smiling face who often accompanied Nan was not my grandad, but my Spirit guide.

Dad told me years later that I probably remember people coming to see me in my pram so vividly because Mum left me in it all day. He said when he came home from work he would get me out of the pram and look after me; I've never really understood why Mum left me in the pram so much.

We lived in a 3-bedded council house in Slough – Eve always says she was 'dragged up in Slough', but actually it was a much nicer place in the '50s and '60s than it is now. Basically, a town with a growing 'trading estate' for low paid manual workers, who, after the war, were happy for anything they got. It was obvious though, that our family were poor even by these standards.

The lasting memory of my childhood is one of hunger. Even today I remember it very clearly. More often than not I could not sleep for thinking about it; I could not be happy or sad, and I could not feel love or kindness. Neither could I feel secure, safe, warm or comforted. Never at peace, always there was the gnawing, all consuming hunger, overshadowing every other thing in my life.

Dad was in and out of work for most of my childhood, but did sometimes hold a job for a year or so. One of these was a rubber mouldings company right in the heart of the trading estate. Mum only ever worked at three part-time jobs that I can recall. The first, when I was four years old, was working the 6pm – 10pm shift on the production line at the same rubber mouldings company Dad worked for; then, as a dinner lady at my primary school, and lastly, as an assistant in a transport café when I was a teenager.

Soon after Mum had started working there, Dad had one of his rare wins on the 'gee-gees', and with this and the extra money Mum was bringing in, Dad bought our first car. It was a very old Morris complete with starting handle and running boards! He said, "I can now pick Mum up from work at 10pm so she won't have to walk home in the dark." He was very proud of his car, and we all enjoyed just sitting in it, I can still remember the smell of old leather and wood.

Joe slept in the smallest bedroom on his own at this time. Eve and I were in a bigger front bedroom, and shared a double bed, as in fact we did until we left home. We were both very uneasy, but for different reasons, when we heard Dad leave the house to go and get Mum from work. Eve said it was the most likely time the ghosts would come and get us; although I did not understand she would not believe me when I tried to tell her Nan was here anyway. We devised a game to take our minds off of having been left; we would talk through where we thought Dad was in the car, all the way to collecting Mum and back. We knew the route to the rubber mouldings factory and we almost always got it spot on – just as Eve said, "They are turning into Chiltern Drive," we heard the car coming down the road. Then, and only then, could we try and sleep.

Mum wanted to go to the work's Christmas party, but Dad did not. They never went out, but the Christmas party included free food and drink for all employees of the rubber mouldings company. Mum was ten years younger than Dad; she thought it would be a laugh, and it wouldn't cost anything. Dad never liked that sort of thing, and, in any case, who would look after the kids?

"Well I'm blinking well going on my own then; you stay and look after them!" Mum shouted, and slammed the front room door behind her as she stormed upstairs.

Dad was upset too, and went to peel some potatoes in the kitchen; he couldn't help but hear Mum crying inconsolably upstairs in their bedroom. He told us kids to stay downstairs whilst he went up to speak to Mum. Eve, Joe and I sat on the bottom of the stairs in silence listening to them argue. I always remember feeling sick with worry whenever I heard raised voices – it usually meant trouble.

"Go away Arthur," she screamed. "I'm fed up with this awful situation. I know we can't afford to go out and I never complain about it, but this is a free night and all my friends on the 6 – 10 shift are going – why can't we?"

"What's so special about these friends? Who are they to you anyway?" Dad was obviously cross, and possibly felt bad about not ever taking Mum out, but it was unusual to hear him shout and we all looked at each other, scared about what might happen next.

"They're not special to me – I just want some fun for a change!" Mum was sobbing her heart out again.

There were a few minutes when all we could hear was Mum crying. Joe was sort of wringing his hands together, like a little old lady in fear of her life. Then Dad said, "Oh come on Vi, stop crying, you go to the party with your friends, you know I wouldn't enjoy it anyway."

Mum replied, "Oh Arthur it won't be the same without you – but if you're really sure, I do need a night out."

"Of course I'm sure, you deserve it love. I'm sorry, I wasn't thinking."

"And I'm sorry too Arthur, gis a kissy kissy," said Mum.

All of us on the bottom of the stairs felt relieved – the shouting and crying had stopped so we had to creep off the stairs very quietly and go into the front room. We all sat on the settee bolt upright still hardly daring to breathe for what seemed like ages. Joe's snotty nose ran down to his lips, and we still sat there until we heard Dad come downstairs and go into the kitchen to continue peeling the potatoes.

We could hear Mum upstairs singing, everyone was happy, and Christmas was coming...

Christmas 1962 was the same as any other Christmas as a child in the Lennox family house. One of Dad's old, worn, long socks each, almost see-through at the heels – so we could guess the last item in there was an apple. It was placed on the end of our beds in readiness for Father Christmas to come down the chimney and quietly creep up the stairs to fill our 'stockings'.

There was always a bright coloured cracker sticking out the top of Dad's old sock in the morning. Our excited hands pulled one thing after another out of our stockings. Always a few nuts, a small packet of sweets, a satsuma, a small car or doll and, finally, an apple in the foot. What joy we had, all the weeks of build up to Christmas and at last it was Christmas morning!

Once we had finished ransacking our stockings we went and woke Mum and Dad up, and asked if we could go down to see if Father Christmas had left us any presents. Eve and I had been told which end of the settee our presents would be left on the night before, and that Joe's would be in an armchair.

Ten minutes later it was all over for another year, and I had already eaten my apple! Our presents were always very similar; we all had a dot-to-dot or colouring book, wax crayons in a little packet, another sweet, a dolly for us girls and a truck for Joe. We were always given a joint present of a

Compendium of Games by Father Christmas, and Dad would try to teach us all how to play Ludo or Drafts, even Chess when we were older, on Christmas afternoon. We loved Christmas; it meant definite food, a sweetie, and not just Dad there all day but Dad playing games with us all afternoon!

1963

In the spring of 1963, a couple of months before my fourth birthday, I met Annabelle and Katherine for the first time. They both became very special friends to me; they seemed to know me, how I was feeling and what I was thinking, sometimes before I knew myself. They helped me through my childhood like only best friends can.

Katherine, Annabelle and I played endlessly – they especially liked Ring-a-Roses, we played it for hours. Mum said I was mad playing Ring-a-Roses by myself. "You're a very odd child!" she said. I just thought she was mad as I wasn't alone.

My Nan liked Annabelle and Katherine, and all four of us would go flying together, it was great. I believed this was a kind of dream that I often had, and it was not until somebody asked me about out-of-body experiences when I was twelve years old, that I realised this was what had happened to me. Things being what they were I could not tell anyone I had these experiences regularly. In fact I was in my late twenties before I even mentioned it to Eve. Although she believed, she still felt frightened by Spirit and did not want to listen to me.

Mum and Dad had a massive row a week or two after my fourth birthday, August 1963. All three of us kids were crying. Mum was heavily pregnant at this time and was shouting and throwing things. Dad was shouting back at her. Dad looked so very upset and so sad; I wanted to cuddle him, but their anger frightened me. We were all told to go to bed, but I don't think any of us slept much – they argued into the night. Something in Dad changed after that argument: he was never quite the same again. It was as if a light went out in his soul.

Dad sold his old car and left the rubber mouldings company shortly after this argument in the August. He got a job at a well-known sweet factory on the trading estate. It was good in that Dad seemed happier working with chocolate rather than rubber. Also, every Thursday he bought cheap chunks of sweets from the staff shop – which really was a treat for us kids – even though the sweets often looked deformed, having no doubt fallen in blobs onto the factory floor before setting and being scraped up – it was good fun and tasty!

Andy was born, at home, September 21st – 9 months to the day since Mum went to the rubber moulding's Christmas party.

1964

Later on, Dad went onto nights at the sweet factory – it was more money and the added bonus was that he was about in the day to look after us and to take Eve and Joe to school. Mum was always tired, and often stayed in bed until 2pm.

We always had to go to bed early when Dad was on nights. We often heard a knock at the door but when we shouted downstairs, "Who is it Mum?" she would only reply, "No one, now go to sleep."

One night after the door had been knocked, Eve and Joe told me to go downstairs and get a drink of water from the kitchen. I could not reach the tap, but I didn't really want to get into trouble. I was on my way back empty handed, and I hesitated at the bottom of the stairs. I was just thinking should I ask Mum to get me a drink or not, when I heard a noise like someone trying to breathe; it got louder and frightened me. I thought Mum must have hurt herself and called out to her as I opened the front room door. I was frozen to the spot by what I saw.

There was a man lying on top of my Mum, and they were both making very strange choking noises. I really felt shocked and unable to move until Mum screamed at me, "Get back upstairs you awful child!"

Then I moved and tore back upstairs as fast as I could. Eve and Joe were shouting excitedly, "Who is it, who is it, is it Uncle Charlie?"

I was shaking and confused: I just said, "I dunno." What I did know, even at that young age, was that it was not right.

That was not the first or the last strange man to come to our house at night when Dad was at work. However, it all stopped when Dad left the factory for another day time job, unfortunately so did the sweets.

Dad was a strict Catholic, and Mum became a Catholic so as to marry him. As kids we were taken to Mass every Sunday by Dad – though this tailed off a lot after Andy was born. Dad had an inner belief that all the pain and hurt could not destroy and although the light in him had dimmed it never went out completely.

About this time I would often hear noises coming from the loft. I know Eve experienced the same, but we did not discuss it till much later on in our childhood. They could be heard from anywhere in our house. I now know this was 'negative' Spirit just having fun trying to scare us. It could be described as a scratching sound, but it was more than that, it was a heavier, dragging sound as if things were being moved around in the loft – when no one was up there.

This is not an unusual place for negative Spirit to be. Often since adulthood, when I have been to clear houses of unwanted Spirit, I have found them to be hiding out of sight in the loft. For some reason they seemed to think that I wouldn't know they were there. But, of course, my guides never fail me, so they always told me where they were. Sometimes it would be 'in the garage' or 'in the basement' or 'out in the shed', but most often 'up in the loft'.

Eve and I would be scared stiff to go up the stairs in our house: whenever possible we would go up together. There was a dreadful feeling up there: especially the landing, underneath the loft hatch, and the toilet, which was directly opposite the top of the stairs. Neither of us could wait to finish on the toilet, especially if we were on our own. Sometimes the noises from the loft would start just as you started to pee, sometimes not, but the threat was ever present – the threat of evil, bad and scary monsters, or ghosts just waiting to pounce on you. We would never dream of shutting the toilet door – knowing if we did the ghost would be right in front of our eyes when we opened it again. In any case, we needed to try to keep our eyes on the loft hatch and the top of the stairs for ghouls, whilst emptying our bladder.

It was absolutely terrifying, and we would run to the top of the stairs and practically throw ourselves down them as quick as possible to get away from the fear behind.

Another strange place in our house was the pantry in the kitchen. The pantry was situated next to the sink, where we all had our morning wash. We used to share one bowl of warm water, which had been heated in a saucepan on the gas cooker.

There was a small rectangular mirror screwed to the door and Mum would use it to put her make-up on, Dad for his shave.

When I was a bit older I always saw shadows of Spirit walking behind me when I looked in that mirror. The pantry itself did not have a good feeling either, not as scary as the loft and landing but eerie nonetheless. I did not like to open it, as I always felt there might be something lurking in the darkness at the back: a feeling that was found to be justified later on in my youth. However, due to the constant lack of food in the house, there was rarely any need to open the pantry anyhow.

At these times, the kind and smiling man I thought was my grandad would come and reassure me that I was safe and that he would take care of me.

We never had running hot water in our house, so we washed downstairs to save taking boiling water, in a wobbly handled saucepan, upstairs to the bathroom. Apart from that, the bathroom sink never had a plug in it.

However, a tin bath was filled up with water every Sunday evening and put on top of the gas stove to heat up. Dad took the water up in saucepans to empty into the bath upstairs. This meant that once a week we had a shallow bath of warmish water. One week the girls would be first in – the next week it was the boys first. The kitchen walls would always be soaking wet with condensation after heating up the tin bath. Because Mum and Dad were heavy smokers, the painted walls of the kitchen had brown streaks of water running down them – nicotine rivers that made our house stink more than usual on a Sunday evening.

One spring day, in 1964, I recall playing in our back garden, a few feet from the back kitchen window, with a plastic ball of Joe's. Joe was at school, as was Eve, and Andy was in his cot upstairs. I had been trying to throw the ball against the six inch square concrete post that supported one end of our washing line. As I was not even five years old my accuracy was not what I would have liked it to be. Hence I kept missing the post and having to go and retrieve the ball from the other side of the garden to try again. I continued this game for some minutes then one time, when I turned back towards the concrete post, I saw a boy, about five or six years old. He was wearing grey shorts and a white/grey shirt. Although he looked a little scruffy I believed this was his school uniform. It did not feel strange to me that he suddenly appeared, it seemed natural and like he was meant to be there.

I said, "Hello, what's your name?"

"I am Will, can I play catch ball with you?" he asked.

"Yeah if you want, you stand up the path a bit and I'll stay by the post," I instructed.

He obediently walked a few steps up the path away from me and turned ready to play. When we began I noticed the cuffs on the sleeves of his shirt were very worn, and every time he went to catch the ball I caught sight of a long length of cotton hanging from his right cuff. I wanted to pull it off for him or at least mention it to him, but something stopped me doing so. We were quite successful at playing catch, even I didn't drop the ball much. Will did not say a lot, but after a while a small smile could be seen on his face.

Eventually Mum was at the back door calling me in to go and get Eve and Joe from school. I turned to Will and shouted, "Bye Will," as I headed indoors.

He said, "Goodbye Susan."

Mum looked at me without expression and just said, "Odd child."

I started school myself in September. Eve's old uniform was a little big for me, but I don't think anyone noticed. Actually I don't think anyone noticed me at all. I stayed as quiet as possible to avoid trouble – Mum had made it quite clear that anything I said or did was just a nuisance, and I thought I would get into trouble at school if I made my presence felt. Besides, Annabelle and Katherine were with me, and we had some fun watching the other kids play from the corner of the playground.

Eve had already moved up to the juniors by the time I started school as she was four years older than me. Joe was in the older class, but he had enough to contend with being so small and being bullied relentlessly, so he couldn't concern himself with me. Eve occasionally came down the side of the infants' playground that was separated from the juniors by iron railings. She would wave to me and when I went over to her she held my hand tight through the bars. When she asked, "Are you OK?" I just nodded, and then her bell would go and she had to leave me anyway.

I recall one particular Parents' Day when Mum came to see my infant teacher about how I was doing at school.

"Hello, Mrs Lennox isn't it?" said Miss Frith my teacher. "Didn't I have Joe in my class a couple of years ago?"

"Yes, yes that's right you did, how is Susan getting on then?"

"Fine, quite well really, although she is very quiet she seems to understand most things," my teacher said.

"Can I look at her work then; what has she been learning lately?" Mum enquired.

We were at the back row of the class, by my desk, and the teacher opened the flip top to my desk. Inside was one green exercise book, half a red and dirty crayon and a six inch ruler that I had got as a birthday gift.

Mum opened my book. It had one and a half lines written at the top of the first page, written, rubbed out, and re-written several times 'My name is Susan, I come from Pakistan and…' That was it. Mum went spare.

"Is this it?! Is that all?! What has she been doing?! What has she learnt?!" Mum's voice was getting louder and more excited as she shouted at the teacher.

All the kids turned to look at us at the back of the class – it was the first time I ever felt exposed – out in the open – noticed! But it was awful. I was thinking, 'Please Mum, don't make it worse.'

Mum liked being the centre of attention, and continued, "So are you telling me because of all the foreigners my daughter will be held back in her education?!"

"Please, Mrs Lennox it's not like that, it has nothing to do with where children come from – it's just that I can only teach at the rate the slowest child can understand."

I was one of three English children in my class: the other thirty-one were predominantly from Pakistan. It was some years later before I heard the word 'racist', and a while later than that before I understood what it meant. My mother, I realised, was definitely a racist. After Mum's original, so-called, horrified outburst (for which she received the attention she craved) she did nothing about the fact her child may have been held back. I don't think she even told Dad.

I believe Dad was in denial about how his children went without food most of the time, and he hid from the truth because he could not deal with it. I believe deep down he knew I was always hungry, we all were. However, Mum used this as a weapon against me. I heard her tell Dad that there was something wrong with me, that the others weren't hungry or at least didn't moan about it all the time.

One day we were all waiting for Dad to come home from work. I was feeling so hungry it made me feel sick, but it was all I could think about. It was pay day and Dad was late again. When he did eventually arrive home he put two pennies and a curled up copy of *The Sporting Life* on the kitchen table.

I hated that paper: it meant Dad had lost his money down the bookies again and we had nothing to eat. Mum and Dad had their usual row. "How can you do this to me and the kids, what sort of life are you putting us through you nasty, nasty selfish man!"

"Vi, I was told 'Golden Boy' was a dead cert, I hoped I could give you all a treat with the winnings, and make it up to you," Dad said in all sincerity.

Mum just packed Andy into his pram, and all four of us kids went with Mum to Nanny's house. It was a five mile walk, but we knew we would all get something to eat when we got there. Mum was crying all the way, nothing we said could console her, so we walked in silence.

That was not the first or last time we had to make that long walk.

CHAPTER 2

1965

When I was six years old they really started. At first it was once or twice a week. Soon I would get messages and visions most of the day every day. At this age I found it hard to differentiate between the living and the dead. One morning, before school, I was making myself a jam sandwich for breakfast. Annabelle was sitting at the kitchen table watching me intently. She said, "Susan, mind you don't use it all, otherwise there won't be enough left for Joe."

I said, "There's loads left for Joe, don't worry," just as Mum walked into the kitchen.

She gave me a strange look and said, "What did you say? Who are you talking to?"

I replied, "It's only Annabelle..." and then realised with horror what I had said. I quickly turned away from Mum's gaze and began furiously eating my sandwich. I was rarely caught talking to myself, so I must have been aware there were differences even then.

The following Saturday night, I remember being woken by a male Spirit about 18 years old. He was throwing playing cards at me one at a time. Not in any malicious or threatening way, but rather to wake me up and to get my attention. He succeeded in waking me, and I felt the temperature in the room drop dramatically as I asked him what he wanted. He just kept throwing the cards and did not speak. I did not feel particularly alarmed (although I was glad Eve was fast asleep), and eventually I snuggled back under the blankets and dropped back off to sleep myself, even though he hadn't left.

A short while after, he woke me again by tapping on my toes. I sat up in bed and asked him, "Who are you, what do you want and why do you keep waking me up?"

He just shook his head from side to side as if he could not explain. He was crying, and his tears ran icy blue down his cheeks. His reply to my question was just 'Friend'.

I said, "I will be your friend, but what's wrong?"

"My Dad hurt me, I couldn't breathe," he replied.

I told him he was safe in my room and that he could stay but I was very tired and needed to sleep. He said no more and I drifted back off to sleep. When I woke, with the sun streaming in and Dad shouting, "Time to get up you lazy lot," he had gone and I never found out what he wanted. I felt bad that I could not keep awake, but I like to think that maybe he just needed to let someone know he was there.

I now know that Spirit need constant reassurance that they can communicate with the living. Whilst growing up I had numerous similar encounters with Spirit, some negative, some positive; it just seemed more frightening when I was young because I didn't understand.

Shortly after the incident with the cards being thrown at me I had one of the most frightening experiences of my childhood. It occurred in my bedroom, and I still wonder to this day if it was because I had assured the boy he would be safe there. Maybe something was offended by my presumption and wanted to punish me for my arrogance. Maybe it was simply to teach me that I was just a girl and I did not know everything about Spirit – not by a long chalk.

I had been in a deep sleep, but awoke very suddenly and was instantly alert. I sensed I should stay still and quiet; my heart thundered as adrenaline pumped through me. I lay in the dark anticipating, waiting, though I did not know what for. My eyes searched all the corners of the room. Eve did not stir, and I presumed she was asleep. It was many years later before I discovered that she too had been awake, lying deathly still and scared to breathe.

I saw a dark shadow next to Eve moving slowly round the bed towards my side. I could hear its breath, deep and rasping with an unmistakable low growl. It was definitely an animal I concluded. As the lumbering shape crept closer I could feel it prodding at the edges of the mattress, snuffling and snorting as it did so. It paused at the foot of the bed, and I was rigid with fear as I felt it pushing at the blankets by my feet.

As it turned the corner and began moving up the bed toward me I could see it more clearly. It looked like a huge wild bear on all fours. I swallowed the scream that threatened to escape from me as I saw it bare its huge, yellowing teeth. Closer and closer to my face – I could see spittle clinging to the fur around its mouth and long strands of saliva hanging from its chin, and dripped periodically onto the floor. It reached the top of the bed, prodded the mattress just under my shoulder and grunted. My eyes stung as they filled with water, and I fought to stop my limbs from shaking. As it began to slowly turn around by my head I felt its hot, wet breath on my face. The stench of rotting meat was overpowering and one I have never forgotten. 'It's going to eat me,' I thought, but it began to creep back the way it had come. Slowly, slowly, tortuously, its huge body passed by me, its belly undulating as it snuffled and snorted, away from me. Will I live? It is going away!

When it had reached the foot of the bed again it stopped and stretched up into a semi-standing position. This is it, I thought, but it appeared to 'jump' three times and then ran headlong towards the built-in wardrobe. It ran right through the closed doors and simply disappeared.

I was so frightened by this seemingly real event, real in the earthly sense, that I became tired and dizzy and non-functioning for weeks afterwards. No one appeared to notice, although Dad said on several occasions something like, "Come on Susie, pull your socks up!" or "You are too slow to catch a cold today love!" The kind and smiling man kept telling me to be brave, to carry on and to remember that I would come to no harm; that he would protect and comfort me. This hardly helped, as I was so terrified and sure that I was either insane or possessed.

However, nothing else untoward happened, and eventually I dared to hope it was all a bad dream, knowing in my heart this was wishful thinking.

One evening Mum asked me and Joe to go scrumping after dark. She told us that there were two or three houses down the road that had lovely big apple trees, one even had a plum tree too. She wanted us to get lots of big juicy, ripe apples for her plan to work. I so wanted Mum to like me, I gladly took up the challenge of, effectively, stealing from our neighbours.

"It ain't really stealing," Mum said, "it's only taking things they ain't gonna know is missing anyway!"

When it got dark Joe and I went armed with old broom handles and a carrier bag. Shaking with excitement and fear we were back home within thirty minutes, our bag full of lovely apples. Mum was very pleased with us, and although this felt very, very wrong it also felt very, very right to me – Mum's approval was a precious commodity indeed! We wanted to eat them there and then, but Mum said she had ideas for them. She said she wanted us to go out in the morning and find as many old lolly sticks as we could find, she was going to make lots of toffee apples!

The next morning we went up and down the road picking up all the old lolly sticks as Mum had requested. We found a total of twenty in all. Mum was already busy making the toffee – it smelt strange, but Mum assured us it would taste great when finished. We washed the sticks in warm soapy water and Mum stuck one in each of the apples. Then, when the toffee mixture was just right, she dipped the apples into it and stood them up on a baking sheet to set.

We had to wait two hours, but it was worth it. They were lovely, it was something to eat and a treat all in one. Mum said we could give the toffee apples out to friends if we wanted. I remember offering one to Sheila Johnson, who was one of the daughters of the 'snobby' family who lived across the road from us.

She said, "Hold on I will have to go and ask me Mum if I can have one."

She skipped off happily enough, but when she returned she looked sullen and upset.

"Mum said I ain't to eat anything from the Lennox house."

Mum heard this and became angry. She shouted, "Trouble with the Johnsons is they think their shit don't stink!" This obviously made an awkward situation worse, and Sheila ran off with tears in her eyes.

We only gave out a couple of toffee apples anyhow. We kept most of them for ourselves. I do remember having a rather crampy tummy for a few days afterwards.

Chiltern Drive ended after our next door neighbour's house and where a field began. It was at this end that the ice-cream man would stop his van to sell ice lollies and ice cream cornets to all the kids down the road. On a dry day there were always lots of children playing in the road or in the field adjacent to it, and when they heard the *Greensleeves* music in the distance they would all run home for some money. My siblings and I would already know whether or not to run home, we always checked before going out to play if there might be a chance of an ice cream that day. Invariably, when one of us asked, "Can we have a lolly today Mum?" the answer would be "No, your Dad is down the betting shop 'cos we ain't got no money." Those days we all stayed where we were, whilst the other kids ran in – Eve, in the middle of hopscotch on the road, Joe playing war games in the field and me sitting in amongst the daisies where the other girls of my age had been chattering away about dolls and prams.

But one particularly hot and unusually humid day Mum said, "Yes OK, you can all have a lolly today when the ice cream van comes around." We couldn't believe our luck, and spent most of the day listening out for the familiar tune to sound. I remember I kept telling my friends I would have a lolly today as well and discussing what type I might get. More than the lolly, delicious as it was, was the fact I felt I belonged, I was normal, one of the crowd. Not different, not bad, not dirty or useless – the feeling of belonging to a group, although it was just a group of children able to buy a lolly, made me feel special.

It was that night that I was woken up by a violent storm outside. Eve was very afraid of thunder and lightning and was hiding under the bedclothes. It did not bother me like that, in fact even now I like to look out at a good storm, I find it fascinating. This night however, I had an extremely uneasy feeling, as if something awful had or was about to happen. This feeling I now call 'The Dreads'. It always precedes something nasty happening, and sometimes I get premonitions of the actual event, but other times it is just like a warning signal for me.

The storm eventually subsided to an occasional, gentle rumble in the distance, almost soothing, and Eve soon dropped off to sleep again.

Then all of a sudden the bedroom door flew open! I thank God that Eve was asleep; she really did not like it when things like that happened.

In walked Mr Hobbs from down the road. He had pyjamas on, which even to a seven-year-old seemed a bit odd in someone else's house. He was grasping the top of his pyjama jacket very tightly with his right hand, and I could see a handkerchief sticking out of the pocket. He came over to my side of the bed and sat down beside me.

I remember feeling bewildered rather than frightened, although there was still an air of unease about.

He grabbed hold of my arm with his left hand. His eyes seemed to be searching deep into my own as he asked, "You can see me, can't you?"

I was dumbstruck and just nodded.

He said, "Please tell Tony I love him and goodbye."

I nodded again, but thought, 'Why can't he tell him himself?' He got up and walked out of my bedroom, and I eventually went back to sleep.

The next morning our neighbour (whom we all called Aunty Mary) came over to tell Mum that Mr Hobbs had died last night in the middle of the storm.

After she left I asked, "Mum what happens when you die?"

She just told me to, "Go away you odd child."

A couple of weeks went by and Aunty Mary came over to our house again. She said to Mum, "Vi, I met Tony, Mr Hobbs' son up the shops this morning. He told me his cat had had eight kittens."

"Aw how cute," I heard Mum say. "How's he doing Mary, it must 'ave been a shock for him."

Aunty Mary said, "He seems to be bearing up quite well actually, now he's on his own. He asked me to ask around to see if anyone would want a kitten."

I stopped doing the jigsaw I was doing and just froze in time. I so wanted a kitten, but I dare not let Mum know that, so pretended not to hear.

"Would you like one Vi?" she asked. "I'm gonna have one for the kids."

"Oh, I don't know Mary, you know, I can't really afford it," Mum replied.

My heart sank.

"He will be giving them away free," said Aunty Mary.

"No, I mean feeding it, sometimes we have trouble buying food for ourselves, let alone a cat."

'That,' I thought, 'was that. Mum won't let us have one.'

Aunty Mary persevered. "Oh, Vi, it's next to nothing, you can get cat food real cheap down the market and the kids would love a pet."

'Yes we would, we would!' I was thinking, whilst still staring at the same piece of jigsaw. In my head I was willing Mum, 'Please, please say yes.'

"Oh, OK Mary, we will take one if it will help Tony out," Mum conceded. "As long as it ain't a ginger tom, I 'ate them blinking things!"

I felt like a prayer was answered! I was so excited and loved the kitten already.

A few weeks later a lovely tabby kitten arrived in a cardboard box. We named him 'Pixie' because he was small, thin and very, very cute.

1966

Mum and Dad were always heavy smokers. Dad was to die quite young with lung cancer, but Mum smoked much more than he did, she was the one who was never seen without a fag hanging out of her mouth. It was on another particularly bad Saturday afternoon (in as much as Dad had lost all our money at the bookies and we had nothing to eat) that Mum called Eve, Joe and I together in the front room. She said she had an important job for us all to do. She pointed at the fireplace. It was Mum and Dad's custom to throw dog-ends into the hearth when they had come almost to the end of a cigarette. Mum wanted us to collect and break open all the old fag ends, and put the leftover tobacco from them into the tobacco tin she had at the ready.

This was to be no mean feat. Due to the severe lack of housework Mum did there was a massive pile of dog-ends in the hearth.

After this long and laborious job, which we all hated because it was so smelly and dirty, we each got a sugar sandwich for our tea and then we were sent to bed. At least Mum and Dad had fags to smoke that evening.

Our house in Chiltern Drive was always busy, at least during the day. Mum's family were a big family in Slough, and her brothers, sisters, nieces and nephews were always coming over, especially her younger brother, our Uncle Charlie. Quite often Charlie would come over when we were about to have our evening meal (if watered down tomato soup and lumpy mash potato can be called a meal).

Mum always idolised Charlie. When he came to our house he would always say, "Hello Violet, have you got any grub on the go love, I'm starved." Of course mum would always offer him some of our meal – which meant we all got less. Not only that, but Uncle Charlie would have so much bread to dip in his soup I remember thinking, 'Please Uncle Charlie, no more or I won't have anything to eat before I go to school in the morning!'

Once Eve was so upset she cried most of the night in bed because she was hungry and Uncle Charlie had pinched some chips off her plate at teatime. I don't think she has ever forgiven or forgotten that.

Uncle Charlie had had several wives but only one child, a boy, when he had one of his longest relationships, which was with Aunty Pat. She had also been married herself before, and already had three kids when she met up with him. He was five years younger than her, and it seems he thought she was a strong mature woman – and he fancied her like crazy.

Aunty Pat was round our house most days – with or without Charlie. Mum and Pat sat drinking tea and smoking roll-ups all day, whilst they nattered, letting all the kids fend for themselves. There was never any structure or routine. If a kid came in hungry they would get whatever there was to eat. Usually there was nothing, and little Andy was often seen to eat dirt, and sometimes worms because he was so hungry. Mum used to laugh out loud and show everyone when he had pooped gravel into his nappy due to his unusual diet. If a kid had injured themselves they got little sympathy and were sent on their way, usually with a sarcastic remark about being a baby – only occasionally, if it were serious, a plaster. Mum rarely did housework, and most of the children on the estate played and fought together in the fields or up and down the road until they were called in for something.

One Saturday afternoon Aunty Pat was round our house drinking tea and smoking fags with Mum as usual. Dad was down the bookies trying to make loads of money so we could eat all week. I think Uncle Charlie was down the pub or 'going to see a man about a dog' which for years I hoped meant we would have a new dog to love, but realised somewhat later it usually meant a dodgy deal of some kind.

I was playing quietly behind the settee with a doll and I heard Aunty Pat say, "How's your kids doing at school then Vi?"

Mum said, "Well Eve has got her 11 plus coming up and I reckon Joe's doing OK, though he's a bit quiet."

"What about your Susan then?" Pat questioned. "She's the one who always seems so quiet."

"Oh, she's an odd one she is," Mum replied. "She talks to 'erself more than she does anyone else!"

"Well I fink that's a bit odd, I mean she's six or seven now ain't she?"

"I know," said Mum, "I keep telling 'er to stop it, she ain't a toddler anymore. You know sometimes I *think* she's possessed or something. Really Pat, sometimes she gives me the creeps!"

"Well, it is possible Vi, I've heard of that 'appening before," Pat almost enthused.

At that moment I stood up from behind the settee. I frightened the life out of the pair of them, they both went pale and swore at me in shock.

I was frightened too, because of their animated and loud reaction to my presence, and I fled upstairs crying. Once again I did not know what I had done wrong.

At about 5.30pm Mum started to 'round up' all the kids, hers and Aunty Pat's, for a plate of chips with brown sauce. I do think that Aunty Pat bringing her kids round and Mum feeding them meant yet again we had less. But Mum was more worried about her friendship with Pat than whether or not her kids were hungry.

Within ten minutes it became apparent that Andy, who was only two years old, and Aunty Pat's Pauline, who was also two, had gone missing. Mum went wild, overacting her anxiety about it, and drawing so much attention to herself that the neighbours almost forgot that small children were missing and very possibly in mortal danger.

The lady across the road who had a phone telephoned the police for Mum, and we all started to search for Andy and Pauline. I felt sick and ran down to the 'Swamp' with Eve, as we both felt they may have gone to water and drowned. Joe started hunting frantically down in the 'Pit' (a large expanse of derelict ground cut out of the surrounding neighbourhood) in and out of brambles, bushes, stinging nettles and thorns. Adults went further afield up and down Chiltern Drive and adjacent roads, telling everyone on the way to look out for two little toddlers in nappies, one a girl and one a boy.

The police arrived at our house and Mum almost fainted in their arms when relaying that she had only taken her eyes off them for a minute! "Oh, my God, my baby!" she cried. In comparison Aunty Pat was very quiet, for a change.

The police went off in their police car with the blue light flashing in search of my baby brother and little Pauline. All Aunty Pat could say was, "Don't fret Vi, let's have a fag and a cuppa."

Eve and I were crying, so frightened at what might of happened to them. No sign of them down the Swamp or the watercress beds. We fully expected to find them face down in the water.

We looked around the area we called 'The Snake Pit' with no luck then we went and helped Joe look in the 'Pit' which was quite a large area. We were shouting their names, almost screaming them, along with an ever growing army of volunteer friends and neighbours.

"Don't worry Mrs Lennox, if you only saw them a couple of minutes ago they can't have gone far," said Mr Baker, the next door neighbour. "We will soon find them I am sure."

Almost thirty minutes later the police car returned with Andy, snotty and crying in the back, and little Pauline looking completely bewildered and obviously in need of a nappy change.

"Oh my God, Andy my baby what happened to you!" Mum screamed.

The rather stern looking copper replied, "We found them a mile away paddling in a stream, goodness only knows how they got across the main road to get there!"

He seemed to be implying somehow that Mum and Pat were at fault. Mum immediately picked up on it and said, "Well thank you officer, I am so grateful my darling baby is safe, it is truly amazing, you turn away for just a moment and they are gone." Then she added for effect, "I don't know how I could ever thank you enough, he is so special to me."

The officer said, "Glad to be of service Ma'am, it may be just as well to lock your gate from now on though."

"Oh, yes Officer, I sure will, they won't get away from us again."

Then one day, just a few weeks after Andy had gone missing, I knew with an absolute certainty that something was protecting me. I was on my own again in the back garden. Some years earlier Dad had concreted in a swing just outside the lounge window overlooking the back garden. He had done this after having a brief door-to-door salesman's job. This entailed him having a Works van and traipsing round posh areas like Datchet and Bourne End trying to sell outside swings, slides, and climbing frames to the rich people for their kids. This was quite a novelty over 40 years ago – but unfortunately did not take off as well as it could have. Or was it just that Dad was not good at selling things? Anyhow, he did not have the job long and apparently accepted the swing instead of wages.

Mum just said, "Well at least the bookies won't take that away."

Anyhow the swing itself had long since broken, and we kids just used the rusting metal frame for climbing on and practising gymnastics.

This was what I was doing when, suddenly, the old poles on one side broke free from the concrete and propelled me through the lounge window. I landed in a shower of glass fragments, some large, some very small. I was totally shocked at first, as were Mum and Aunty Pat, whose feet I had landed in front of just as she was lighting her hundredth fag of the day.

Before anyone could speak I got up and run out of the room and upstairs, hiding under my bedclothes like a frightened rabbit. I was frightened of Mum telling me off for breaking the window, not any other reason.

Sure enough, when Mum gathered herself I heard her screaming, "Susan, Susan where are you?" I kept quiet, then I heard her again – coming up the stairs.

"Susan where are you, have you hurt yourself dear?"

'Dear?' I thought, 'perhaps she isn't angry with me, perhaps she's concerned!'

She entered my room, with Aunty Pat hot on her heels. "There you are silly, have you cut yourself anywhere?"

"Vi, get her out from under them bedclothes, she must have loads 'a cuts, she'll be bleeding all over the bed," Aunty Pat said.

That's when it struck me that I was absolutely fine, not a bump, not a bruise or a cut, in fact not a mark on me.

Mum pulled the clothes off me and gave me a good look all over. "Impossible," she said to Aunty Pat. "I can't see one cut on her."

"Did you hurt yourself anywhere Susan, your head or arm or knee, anywhere?"

"No Mum, sorry I broke the window," I said.

"What do you mean, you must be hurt somewhere?" piped up Aunty Pat again.

I just looked up at Mum wondering what would happen next. She told me to come downstairs and have a cup of tea with them while she cleared up the glass.

Something was protecting me physically and emotionally that day. Mum even put her arm round me briefly when she brought me a cup of tea. "Are you OK love?" she asked.

I did not realise at the time, but the show of affection was all for Aunty Pat's benefit.

1967

A few months went by. One wet and cold Monday afternoon, just after Christmas, Mum got out an old photograph album. She had asked Dad the previous weekend to go up in the attic to get Andy's old cot down – Aunty Pat was pregnant again and did not have a decent cot to put the latest baby in.

Whilst Dad was up there he had come across the album and apparently decided to bring it down to look at. Anyhow, Dad was down the betting shop and Mum gathered us all around her. She sat in the middle of the sofa, with Eve and I on one side, and Joe and Andy on the other. Andy was only three years old and seemed much more interested in wiping his hands on the arm of the sofa to clean off the mess his 'Buppy Crus'[1] had made than looking at photographs. As Mum turned the pages I saw a picture of my grandmother (Dad's mum).

"Look Nan there's a photo of you!" I shouted, pointing to Nan's picture in the album.

Mum was furious. "What do you mean it's your Nan, you ain't never seen her before," she demanded.

"But Mum she's sitting there." I pointed to my Nan who was sitting opposite me.

Mum jumped up and slapped me across the face. "You monster, your Nan is dead, she died before you were born. You're evil to play tricks like that!"

My face stung so bad, but although my eyes filled with tears, I did not let one drop down my cheeks in front of her. She sent me up to my room. "Your Dad won't be so pleased with you when he hears about this."

My Nan followed me upstairs and sat next to me on the bed. She put her arm around me. Between sobs I said, "So you're dead then?"

"Yes," she said.

I just replied, "Oh, OK then," still not really understanding what dead meant. But one thing I did understand that day was that I was different.

---

[1] Buppy Crus is the end slice of a sliced loaf of bread – spread with margarine and cut into squares

Mum came up to my room some time later. She told me in a very matter of fact way that from now on I was going to be known as 'Evil Child' and I must stay put until I said sorry.

When Dad came home, having lost most of his dole money in the bookies again, she told him what had happened and he came up to see me.

I thought he would have been on my side, but he was in a bad mood with me. He said it was wrong to talk to dead people, that I should leave them in peace in heaven, it was only bad people that called them back.

I tried to explain that I didn't ask them to come, they wanted to. He just said, "I've told you not to, so just ignore them!"

I wanted to ask him how you could tell if someone was a dead person, but apart from the fact he was already very annoyed with me, he was halfway out the door.

Anyway, after that I kept most of my spiritual experiences and messages to myself, at least for a while. In a way it was a good thing. The spirits meant I always had someone to talk to, and I certainly could not ignore them like Dad wanted me to. People who were alive did not seem interested in me much anyhow: often they did not seem to know I was even there, and their facial expressions suggested they were looking through or past me.

Most mornings Dad would wake us up and get us ready for school whilst Mum was still in bed. Eve had to leave thirty minutes earlier than Joe and I as she was at secondary school by now.

One morning, just as normal, Dad kissed me and Joe goodbye, and watched us as we made our way down the path and onto the street, crossing to the field adjacent to it. Eventually we got to the main road, the other side of the Pit, which was a much quicker way to our junior school than going right around the council estate. There seemed to be so much traffic this particular morning, much more than was usual. We needed to cross this road to carry on for school; it was taking so long I started to worry that we would be late. Then a lady driver (quite rare in those days) slowed right down to let us cross. I remember her dark curly hair and her red, red lips – she looked like a film star – and most startling of all she was looking straight at me, not through or past me, but at me, she saw me! I told Joe to come with me, but he was too scared and pulled back as I moved forward. Then the lady seemed to think I was going to stay back as well and she accelerated. Time passed so slowly, things happened as if in a dream, but very drawn out. Nan and Katherine and Annabelle were there as well. We did not speak to each other, and yet we communicated a certain strange fear, unreal, but a sense that however long this takes it could end up very badly, and there is nothing any of us can do about it but watch in slow motion. Her car hit me and I flew up into the air and landed on her bonnet, then rolled out into the road. I was so terrified of being hit again that I somehow pulled myself up and hopped to the kerbside.

Dad had been in the kitchen washing up at the sink and watching us from the window when he saw me flying up in the air. It must have been a terrible shock for him.

Next thing I knew, lots of people were shouting, rushing towards me, crowding round me, the film star lady was crying, but my Nan kept saying, "You're alright Susan, you will be alright, I am here love."

51

I started to feel drowsy; I looked up and saw Dad was there, holding me close. Joe ran home, crying, to wake Mum up. Dad went with me to hospital and stayed with me all the time.

I remember I had no pain at first although I was feeling queasy. In fact, apart from some soreness when antiseptic spray was used by the nurse on my cuts, I felt nothing until about five hours later. From then on I realised shock can be a wonderful thing – it prevents the body from experiencing pain. This has helped my understanding in later life that if someone has a serious accident or injury they probably do not feel the pain at first. This has been confirmed to me numerous times during 'readings' by Spirit who have passed over in this way. I firmly believe everything happens for a reason – who knows, my accident may have been just so I could reassure people later on.

About five hours after the accident, I began to feel lots of pain in both legs, so a nurse gave me some tablets to help. I then seemed to be drifting in and out of sleep. At one point I woke up feeling I was about to be sick. I was hot and sweaty and felt very frightened. Dad was still clutching my hand. I turned my head towards the other side of the bed and immediately felt much calmer. Sitting holding my other hand was the man I had always thought of as my grandad (he always felt like that to me). He smiled and said, "You'll be alright."

I smiled back at him and asked, "Are you my grandad?"

My Dad replied, "No love it's me, your dad, I won't leave you alone."

The man on the other side of the bed replied, "I am your guide, Michael, I am here to help you." Then I drifted back off to sleep.

A little later a nurse came back to my room, which was quite dark as the curtains were shut. Dad was still sitting next to me. She looked straight at my Dad and said, "I'm sorry Mr Lennox, but the x-rays show that Susan has broken her legs."

Dad was still holding my hand, and he squeezed it hard when he heard this.

Later I heard the nurse telling Dad that the doctor thought I was anaemic and malnourished. They suggested I ate a lot of greens for iron and be encouraged to eat more to fatten up a bit!

When I was allowed home from hospital, it was with both legs in plaster and in the back of an ambulance. Dad was still with me. I had instructions to rest in bed until I was better. When I got home, Mum and Aunty Pat were waiting for me. Mum gave me a kiss on the cheek. Dad said, "Vi, the hospital said she must rest in bed. They said it will be more painful in a day or so once the bruising comes out, but hopefully she will feel much better in a week or two."

Mum gestured to the bed she had made on the sofa and said, "She don't need bed, we can see her and look after her better down here." So I went on the sofa and got no rest due to a house full of kids (mainly Aunty Pat's) and friends and relatives popping in and out to see me and my funny looking legs. The plaster had been applied from top to bottom on both legs, and David Jones, a friend of Joe's, said I looked like half an 'Invisible Man'. This was a television programme that depicted a man who was invisible, and the only time you could see him was when he covered himself in bandages.

All the neighbours bought me sweets, and one lady bought me a bottle of Lucozade, which was very expensive and made me feel a little special. Also my nanny, my mum's mum gave me a present, the only present she ever gave me – it was a china doll, a year older than my mum. It was lovely and I called it Baby. I will keep it forever, and give it to my daughter when I die.

A few days later, Aunty Pat bought me a packet of small sugar coated jelly sweets. She said, "'Ere kiddo, try these new special sweets for a special girl," as she tossed them into my lap. They were indeed new on the market and recently advertised on television. They looked really colourful, but I still felt sick, and I just fell asleep with the packet in my hands. I have never been able to have one of those jelly sweets to this day, because it brings back vivid memories of feeling sick and being in pain.

I woke up to a very heavy, thick smell of cigarette smoke just as Mum said, "'Ere Pat 'ave another fag." Mum looked at me and back to Aunty Pat, and said, "Do you want another cuppa Pat?"

"Oh yeah ta, Vi," she replied.

"Do you want one love?" Mum asked me.

"Yes please." I felt quite grown up at that moment.

During that particular cup of tea Aunty Pat started asking Mum questions like, "How long is she going to be like this?" and "Shouldn't she be exercising more or she'll go stiff?"

I was in a lot of pain, especially at the top of my legs where the plaster rubbed, without trying to move too soon. However, Mum and Aunty Pat thought I should help myself, by insisting I walked the length of the room – "For your own good dear, so you can go to the toilet on your own."

They made me get up and do it. I felt shooting pains from my feet right up my legs, and then continuing to my shoulders with every movement. The pain was so intense the tears rolled down my face, but I wasn't crying – my eyes just watered with the pain.

Mum shouted, "Don't be such a baby. I'll have to get you a pram in a minute!"

This was three days after I had been run over, but it was obvious Mum had had more than enough of looking after me.

Two weeks later I was taken back to school, with the plaster still on both legs. I hardly made it walking that far, but at least Mum walked with me: usually I went on my own with Joe.

It was a nightmare – I was crying and pleaded with Mum at the school gates not to make me go in. I was in pain, and the top of my legs were chafed and starting to bleed where the plaster had rubbed because of walking so far. She just turned and walked away.

I stumbled down to the playground like a zombie, legs apart and in agony. When the bell went, Joe, who had promised Mum he would keep an eye on me, had to go to the upper playground to get to his classroom.

The ensuing rush to form an orderly queue for my classroom, which was adjacent to the lower playground, meant, inevitably, I was knocked to the ground.

It was added pain to that I was already experiencing and I screamed out. A teacher came and helped me up, I was taken into an empty classroom and I sat down on the edge of a chair.

It seemed I was left alone forever. I was hurting all over, and I began to think, I'd been forgotten, when the door opened. Mr Hillington, the headmaster, and Mum came into the room.

Mum ran up to me saying, "Oh, my poor darling, what happened. I told you, you shouldn't go back to school yet!"

"Well yes Mrs Lennox, as I said in the office, we feel Susan is far from ready to attend school at the moment. The school nurse advises that she does not attend school again until at least after having the plaster removed," said Mr Hillington.

Mum said, "Oh, quite right Mr Hillington, I agree, kids eh!" She grabbed my hand and could not get us out of the room fast enough.

Mum did keep me off school until after the plaster was removed from my legs and I was able to walk normally. I remember during those weeks at home, whilst I was recovering, Mum showed me how to do some 'cooking'. This really only stretched to peeling and chipping spuds, and one day warming up a tin of soup. However, I so enjoyed this, mainly because I was getting some attention from Mum, but I also felt proud to be able to peel potatoes, to be helping out – perhaps I wasn't useless after all? I remember being particularly disappointed one day when I asked if I could make some jam tarts, because Mum just said, "If we had some jam you could, but we ain't." This bothered me for some days as I so wanted to make tarts to look like the ones I saw in my nursery rhyme book. At the time I thought Mum could easily get some jam if she wanted, but actually I now believe we really could not afford even that.

Mum knew we were all hungry most of the time, goodness only knows we told her often enough. I was particularly skinny at this age and always very tired. One morning in the school holidays Mum got us all up and ready to go out. We did not know where, but it made a nice change for us to be going out and for Mum to get up so early. Mum let me wear Eve's cardigan as it was a bit chilly in the morning air.

When I asked her where we were going, she just said to the doctors. I secretly hoped this might mean a sweetie on the way back: the doctor's surgery was a long walk away but near lots of shops.

When we walked into the doctor's, Mum went up to the receptionist, and I heard her say, "I have an appointment with Doctor Bertram for my daughter Susan." I looked at Mum in total surprise as I knew I felt fine: I wasn't ill. We were called in almost immediately, Mum and I, and the others stayed in the waiting room.

Mum looked upset, and said to the doctor that she was very worried about me. He asked what the problem was, and she said that I would not eat, no matter what she put in front of me. The most she could get me to eat was a small mouthful, she told him. I could not understand what Mum was talking about. I was always starving hungry and ate everything that I was given. Sometimes it was a teaspoon of mash and a couple of peas, but I would even lick the plate I was so hungry. Why would she say such a thing?

The doctor turned to me, and said that I had to eat everything my mother gave me to eat.

I said, "I do."

He was not listening to me and continued, "Well, it's naughty not to eat, your poor mother is worried sick!"

I started crying. I could not explain that it was not like that, that I longed for a real meal to fill me up.

He turned back to Mum, who by this time had a smile on her face. "Don't worry Mrs Lennox, she will eat when she wants to, some kids are naturally skinny."

With that Mum got up and said, "Thank you Doctor, goodbye." Then we left.

A week or so after I had been taken to the doctor's, a very well-to-do and posh looking lady came to our house. Mum told us an important lady was coming to see us and we must behave ourselves. Mum worked cleaning the house all morning, even washing the sticky kitchen floor. When she arrived I was very disappointed because she was not the queen or even a princess. She had a woollen suit on and heavy framed glasses. She spoke with all the family, and Mum offered her a cup of tea. She had prepared a tray ready, but the lady said, "No thank you."

At one point she asked me what I had for breakfast, and I told her, "Daddy's sauce sandwich." She nodded and smiled at me, and then I wasn't scared of her anymore.

A few weeks later the Lennox children started receiving free school meals.

It was so good to eat properly at least once a day, but it only served to make my siblings and me stand out even more than we already did in our classes at school. It was very rare for children to get free school meals in those days, and every Monday morning all the other children would queue up to pay the teacher their dinner money. They all stared at me when the teacher said, "Susan Lennox, free," as I was the only one who remained in my seat.

We were all picked on, to some extent, because of it. I did not understand what I had done to be so different – I felt as if something was against me – but I could no more express that than walk on the moon. I now believe it was just children being children, and the fact they notice anybody a little out of the ordinary.

At least when the summer holidays came we had some respite from the bullies, but our bellies were empty for six weeks without the free school meals.

CHAPTER 3

After my accident, life seemed to be more difficult for me: bad thoughts and unkind people were everywhere. I also had numerous encounters with Spirit. Our house seemed to attract Spirit, and although most were good, occasionally they were unpleasant. The September of 1967 was unusual in that they were particularly negative towards me.

One afternoon, on returning home from school, I had the Dreads again. I was sure something bad was about to happen. The feeling continued until bedtime. When I got into bed I confided to Eve that I felt worried about something but didn't know what. Eventually, I dropped off to sleep, but it was only for a couple of minutes, because I jumped out of my skin when someone began laughing out loud – it was a horrible, sinister laugh.

I could then feel something moving under the covers; terrified, I forced myself to look. I pulled back the blankets and saw hundreds of snakes squirming all over me and Eve. I let out a scream, which made Eve jump up and get out of the bed and made the snakes disappear.

I could not believe it. I searched all round the room to try and see where they had gone – but there was no sign of them. Eve said she did not see or feel anything. She said it must have been a dream, but it was so real I know it was not just in my mind.

I asked Eve not to tell Mum or Dad because they would get cross.

Three nights later I was awakened from a deep and restful sleep by Eve frantically hitting me. I sat bolt upright, heart pounding from such an abrupt awakening. "Eve!" I cried, "What is wrong?" She was still hitting me with one hand, and pointing with the other to the wall at the foot of the bed. She looked as though she was trying to scream, but what came out was more like a high-pitched squeak.

I looked at the wall and jumped up out of bed. At first I thought my tired eyes were playing tricks on me, as I could not believe what I saw. What looked to be blood was pouring down the wall. It was as though the house was living flesh and had severed an artery. The thick, deep-red liquid was haemorrhaging from the wound at an alarming speed. The air was filled with that familiar unnatural chill and a cloying coppery smell that was overwhelming. It was as though we had awoken from our sleep to find ourselves in the middle of a horror film. I tried my best to calm Eve down.

"It's not going to hurt us and it's not getting any closer," I said, trying to lessen her fear.

It was cold comfort to a girl who had just awoken to find her bedroom looking like a theatrical massacre. She could hardly speak and just said, "Mm… Mm…make it go away!" She was visibly trembling.

I was shaking myself as I approached the wall, the rushing sound of the waterfall of blood in front and Eve's whimpering behind me. I looked down at the floor, and was taken aback to see that there was no blood on it. Where was it all going? It seemed to stop just short of the skirting board and simply disappear. I could not make any sense of it.

"It can't be real, Eve," I said, "look, it doesn't reach the floor, there is not one drop on the floor!" Eve did not want to look closer; she pulled the bedcovers up under her chin.

"I ain't going near it, real or not!" she cried.

"Well, sitting here staring at it ain't helping anything," I replied. I swallowed hard and reached out my hand to touch it. As soon as my finger made contact, it just disappeared.

We stared at the wall for a long time in disbelief. I got back in bed and asked Michael to tell whatever it was that had caused it to go away. The temperature in the room returned to normal. Eve was still beside herself, and we held hands very tightly. She was extremely on edge, and asked that we keep holding hands. She squeezed my hand and then I squeezed hers in reply. It seemed to reassure Eve, and we kept on doing this in a rhythmic pattern until we fell asleep. The next morning when we awoke, we were both still squeezing each other's hand alternately.

For many weeks after this, Eve and I went to bed and held hands until we fell asleep.

1968

I was playing over the field with my little brother Andy and my two best friends Annabelle and Katherine. It was a hot summer day and the grass seemed taller than ever this year. We had been collecting daisies to make a daisy chain for about twenty minutes then we decided to make our usual camp. To do this we had to roll around in the deep grass to flatten it and make a definite perimeter wall, then no one else could see us or even guess we might be there.

We sat making daisy chains and chatting. I was eating handfuls of grass, between selecting the prettiest of the daisies, because I felt so very hungry. The last thing I had eaten was a brown sauce Buppy Crus, the afternoon before. We were talking about what we would be doing next when suddenly the sky grew dark – black even. I turned to the others and shouted, "Quick, it's going to rain, we are going to get soaked, we'd better run!"

Annabelle said, "Don't worry, take no notice…" but then her voice faded and I could not hear her any longer. Her voice was replaced by the ominous and growing sound of rhythmic marching. I started to panic, because I could not see Annabelle, Katherine or, to my horror, Andy, even though I still had a tight grip on my little brother's sweaty hand. I could hear banging and what sounded like gunfire in the distance.

The marching was getting ever nearer; as it did so, the smell of gunpowder became stronger, too. Then a hazy smoke, which was stinging my eyes, was all around me, and I saw hundreds of soldiers going past. They were all over the place, but not one of them looked at us. I felt absolutely terrified and wanted to go home, but when I looked in the direction of home it was not there! I was very confused. Then, through the smoke, I saw the familiar face of Michael and felt very calm. He told me to sit down in the grass again. I said we really should go home. Then I clearly saw Annabelle again, sitting in the sunshine. Her voice got louder and louder until it was at a normal pitch. She was still nattering about what we should do later. Bless her, Annabelle could talk for England. I pulled at my brother and friends and ran home.

When I reached home I told Dad what had just happened. He said it must have been my imagination, but I insisted it was not. He said, "Well, you must have fallen to sleep in the sun and dreamt it, or worse still you are the reason they came."

I didn't know what he meant; I just felt like I was in the way.

The following weekend it was my friend, Teresa's birthday, and she was having a party at her house. She had invited me and I couldn't wait. Mum had bought a box of chocolates to wrap up so that I could give her a present.

The party was great, so much food. I had two sandwiches, a fairy cake, and jelly and ice cream. I thought I had died and gone to heaven.

When the parents came to collect their children, Teresa asked me to stay a while and play with her new toys in her bedroom. Her bedroom smelt clean and fresh – and it was tidy. Her dad came up and fixed a mobile that she had been given by an aunty of hers to her bedroom ceiling. It was lovely with pretty butterflies and birds hanging at various levels around it.

Once he had done it, her dad said, "Just half an hour now Teresa then Susan will have to go home." He smiled at me as he left the room: he was a nice man.

"OK Dad," she said.

We played with her new dolls: one had long blonde hair and a blue gingham dress, and I really wanted a doll like it. Anyway, Teresa let me play with her the most even though it was brand new. Teresa dressed up in her new pink, sparkled, high-heeled plastic shoes, together with pink earrings, necklace and ring, and a very bright pink feather boa to complete the look. She reminded me of a princess. Quite suddenly, a gust of wind blew through me. We both looked up at the mobile which was whizzing round. I had the urge to turn around, and as I did

I looked toward the open bedroom door. There was a girl with long straight black hair and a full length white party dress on just standing in the doorway. She seemed very cold and looked terrified, and then I realised she was dripping wet." She needs a towel," I said to Teresa.

"Who?" she said.

Then The Dreads hit me. I hadn't even realised she was dead: the vision was in black and white, but it had not struck me at first.

"Oh, no one," I replied to Teresa.

In my thoughts I asked her what had happened. She just pointed out of the bedroom window. I turned to the window but could see nothing unusual. When I turned back to speak to her again she had gone.

The mobile slowed down and the cold wind blowing through me began to ebb away.

The next thing I knew Teresa's dad was shouting up the stairs. "Susan will have to go now love, you have to have your bath and get ready for bed."

This seemed to focus my mind with a jolt, and I realised what I had just seen was not normal. I started to hurry down the stairs as I said goodbye to Teresa. She said, "Hold on Susan, I want you to take a fairy cake home." In my haste to get away I almost declined. However, although I had already had cakes today, they were such a rare treat I waited. She wrapped a cake that had pink icing and silver balls on the top, in a napkin and gave it to me.

I said, "Ta, see you tomorrow." I ran out of her house and across the road as fast as I could.

When I got inside my front door, Dad was there and asked, "Was it a nice party love?"

"Great thanks, Dad," I replied, and ran upstairs to my bedroom. I sat alone on my bed, holding my fairy cake for ages. I was trying to make some sense of what I had just seen, what had just happened to me in Teresa's bedroom. I felt helpless (how could I tell anyone?) and frightened (what if it happens again?).

I kept thinking there must be some reason for it. Perhaps I was imagining these things. Was I somehow supposed to help these people? Had I done something wrong? Was I being punished for something? I just could not understand.

Negative Spiritual activity was definitely happening more frequently around this time. A week or two after Teresa's birthday party, I lay awake in bed trying hard to fall asleep – I could see spirit lights all around me. I had the strong sense that there was something important they wished to communicate to me. I closed my eyes and suddenly found myself standing in someone's front garden. It was a weird sensation, which at once felt both surreal and completely natural. I knew that I was not dreaming. I knew that I was still in my bed in Slough, although what I was seeing around me was many, many miles away. Yet I was completely immersed in this vision: its sights, sounds and smells.

I did not recognise the garden or the neighbourhood at all. I could hear someone talking, and I looked towards the house. Two girls stood looking at me. They looked to be about four and six: both wore beautiful pink dresses and had neatly brushed shiny, long, blonde hair. They looked picture perfect, almost like dolls. I waved to them and as I did I heard a door slam at the side of the house. A man came storming out towards the girls, obviously in a very bad mood. He spoke harshly to both of them, completely ignoring me. It dawned on me that whilst the younger girl could see me, the elder girl and the man could not. A shiver scuttled up my arms, and I knew then that it was the young girl who wished to show me something.

As the man called to the girls to go with him the younger of the two turned to me, "Please, come with us," she asked urgently. I nodded and followed behind the trio as they walked for some time, eventually coming to a parade of shops. All three went into a laundrette. As soon as they walked in my stomach hit the floor. I felt an overwhelming sense of dread and began to feel faint, wishing I were back in my bed.

The little girl turned to me, as if sensing that I knew something unspeakable was about to take place. She looked straight at me, her baby-blue eyes fixed on mine. "Daddy did it," she whispered, and continued her gaze until I nodded to indicate that I had understood.

The man gave the elder girl a coin and ordered her to go next door to get him a paper. As she left the laundrette I almost followed her. It was dark outside and the area seemed to be a bit rough. I was worried something was going to happen to her, but the young girl touched my arm gently and shook her head. I was to stay put.

What I saw next shocked me and has stayed with me my whole life. The man violently grabbed the young girl by one arm, using his other hand to thump her repeatedly in the stomach and head. At first she screamed, but it soon fell to a sob. He shouted at her, his face right next to her, "You are a BAD, BAD girl!!" He was in such a frenzy and, as he shouted, spit from his mouth sprayed the helpless, tear-soaked child.

I felt hot tears sting the back of my eyes. I wanted to grab her, hug her, run away with her, but I was paralysed. I thought it was over, but then my blood ran cold when I realised he had not yet finished. He picked up the girl who by now lay sobbing in a crumpled heap on the stark, cold floor of the laundrette. He opened the door to one of the huge tumble dryers and bundled her in, slamming the door shut on her with such force it made a sickening clunk as it closed. She looked straight at me, her face twisted with terror, the once immaculate hair dishevelled and blood running from her mouth. She put her hand up against the glass door as if reaching for help. I tried and tried to scream, but no sound came out as I saw the man reach for the power button and switch it on.

Instantly I was back in the bedroom, struggling to breathe (I had involuntarily been holding my breath as I watched the girl's ordeal). I was worried sick about her, but I knew I couldn't tell anyone. I would only get in trouble and what good would it do? I had no idea where the incident had taken place.

A few days later I heard on the news that a little girl had been murdered in a laundrette by her father who had stuffed her into a tumble dryer. I think it was in the USA. I cried and asked that I not be shown such awful things if I had no way of preventing them. That beautiful little girl has never left my memory.

However, I have continued to have premonitions throughout my life.

In October 1968 I had a horrible day at school. I was worrying about all the family but in particular about our cat Pixie. I kept feeling he was trapped and hurt and no one could help him. I expected to hear he was missing when I got home and sure enough no one had seen him all day. Dad said he was probably just playing with his other cat friends, but I knew he was hurt or worse! No one would believe that I knew something bad had happened to him. Pixie often went missing for a few days at a time, either chasing mice or female cats! When after three or four days there was no sign of him, the rest of the family became concerned.

Where Mum had been saying, "Don't worry, he'll come home when he's hungry," she was now saying, "Perhaps he's been run over."

Eve, Joe and I hunted frantically up and down our road and all surrounding areas. We were looking for signs of a dead cat, hoping we wouldn't find one. Several days passed and no sign of Pixie was found. We all began to grieve, worrying about what had happened to him but knowing it wasn't good. Bonfire night had been and gone, and Joe believed he might have been burnt to death in one of the fires.

All four of us children were upset and found when one started crying about Pixie the others would as well. One evening shortly afterwards, when we were all ready for bed, Dad said, "I want you all to sit and watch this film for a while before you go up."

Five minutes later there was a knock at the door. It was Uncle Charlie.

He said, "Surprise, Surprise!" as he walked into our living room with a box that appeared to be wobbling.

Dad had a sparkle in his eyes and said, "Gather round kids." Mum was on the settee, smiling.

As Uncle Charlie opened the box we could see it was a ball of white fluff, a cute puppy. We were all so excited and took it in turns to cuddle it.

"It's for you," Dad said. "You must all look after it."

We were all thrilled and Eve asked, "Is it a girl or a boy?"

Uncle Charlie said, "It's a girl." He went on to explain that our nanny had heard about Pixie and knew someone who was looking for a home for their puppy. Mum and Dad were smiling broadly. We called the puppy Sally – she was gorgeous. She didn't take away the hurt of losing Pixie, but she helped a little.

A week later, Joe's friend Ben Smithson knocked our door to play with Joe. He was surprised to find we had a puppy and asked how long we had had it. Joe told him about Pixie and how he had been missing since before Bonfire night, and that Mum and Dad got us the puppy to take our minds off Pixie. Ben said he remembered seeing some older boys throwing fireworks at a cat down the road from us. He also reminded us that a vet lived opposite to where he had seen these boys torturing a cat, and maybe it would be worth asking him if he knew anything about it. Joe thought it was a good idea, but did not know for sure where Mr Marks the vet lived. They got involved in swapping their cigarette cards and no more was said about it.

Later that evening we had a knock on the door and Mr Marks the vet was standing at our door with Pixie in a cat box. He told us that Ben Smithson had called round and told him the Lennox family were missing a cat. Poor Pixie was frightened in the box, and when Mr Marks got him out we were all shocked to see the burns and scars on him. He had been a beautiful cat. Mr Marks said he had been tortured by some ruffians, and he had been alerted by a local lady of a stray with burns in the area. Mr Marks soon found him and took him in. Although we were all very happy to have Pixie back, we were a bit worried Sally may have to go. Dad soon reassured us all that Sally was here to stay.

A few days after this a reporter from the local *Evening Mail* newspaper came round to our house. He said he had heard about Pixie and would like a photo and more details for the newspaper. Mum fell over herself trying to be nice to him, but he refused a cup of tea as he took in the dirty carpet and sticky tabletop.

Mum tried to put on a posh voice and said, "Joseph go and find your little friend Benjamin and ask him to come here for a photograph for the newspaper man." I remember an awkward silence whilst we all waited for Ben to arrive. Mum tried to engage the young and spotty man in conversation, but he kept writing things down and checking his camera. He was obviously uninterested in anything she had to say. When Ben finally arrived, breathless and with a snotty nose, the reporter took a photo of Joe and Eve holding Pixie with Ben looking on. The headlines read 'Mystery of Missing Pixie Solved'. I was just so happy to have Pixie back – he was very nervous for ages after his ordeal, but he loved and cuddled into me every chance he got.

CHAPTER 4

When I was ten years old, I had some lovely spiritual experiences. This helped to soften the frightening negative ones to a degree.

I recall I would often look up at the planes going over Slough as they were coming in to land at Heathrow Airport. I would be able to see in my mind's eye, the people sitting on the aeroplane. I could see their features, whether they were talking or not – even what sort of age they were. I felt as if I was in a type of trance: seeing these things clearly, while everything else around me was slightly foggy or out of focus.

It was a pleasant sensation and therefore quite a pastime for me at this age. It always felt like a natural, normal thing to do. Some people may have thought I was dreaming or hallucinating. I believed it was Spirit showing me these close-up details, and years later I had this verified when I was on a plane myself heading for America.

I was off on holiday, and about three hours into the flight, when I fell into a trance-like state. Whilst in this state I was being shown pictures of people on the aeroplane. I could still see all the people around me, although they were not in focus. Then one particular couple came to the forefront of my mind. The female, an older woman in a bright-red skirt suit, had dark hair, small eyes, and she was reading a glossy magazine. Next to her was a much younger man – he had the same small eyes but was very attractive nonetheless. He wore a pale-blue woollen pullover. I thought he was her son. I studied them in detail for a minute or two, and then the trance-like state receded and I could see my fellow passengers clearly again.

After a few moments, wondering if anyone had noticed my strange staring, I gathered myself and attempted to look around at other passengers hoping to see this couple somewhere. It did not happen, but the experience took me back to my childhood when I clearly saw images of people sitting in a plane going overhead.

An hour later I needed the toilet, so I got up and headed for the nearest one behind me. This was engaged, so I decided to walk through the curtains to the next. This was also engaged, and I felt that walking about a bit would be a good idea on a long-haul, so pushed through the next set of curtains.

I was stunned, paralysed on the spot for a moment or two, because immediately I got through the curtains I saw the couple from my trance sitting three seats back. The woman peered over her magazine and I noticed her small eyes. She seemed to recognise me, I am not sure, perhaps she was just surprised by my reaction to her and her son.

On the way back from the toilet I heard her ask him, "Do you know that woman?"

This was definitely not a dream or a hallucination; it was based on the premonition I had when I was ten.

Admittedly, at the age of ten, I did have dreams, but these were usually about food.

One afternoon I saw an advertisement on a leaflet that came from a magazine Mum had been given by Aunty Pat. It showed a chest freezer full of lots of lovely food so that the wonderful contents were spilling from the top. It was a competition to win the freezer, but, in my longing for something to eat, I imagined all the scrumptious food would be won by our family. Not only frozen and delicious steak pies, but frozen sprouts, sausages, burgers and the unheard of tub of vanilla ice cream!

I begged Mum to enter the competition; it was mainly a tie-breaker, finish this sentence...*This new, easy to clean chest freezer, is the best product on the market for keeping the whole family happy because*...I could not believe it! All we had to do was write in the rest of the sentence and we would get all that food.

Mum promised that she would enter the competition, but she would need to fill it in when us kids were all in bed so she could think of the best words so she could win. I rushed to bed that night behaving myself and being quiet to let Mum think. I prayed and prayed until I fell asleep that God would help Mum to say the right things so we could all have the food shown on the picture.

The next morning I asked Mum how she did.

"How I did with what?!" she shouted.

"How did you do with the competition?" I asked.

"Oh, Oh yeah I did well, I think we could really win it," she said.

"What did you put Mum?" I persisted.

"I can't remember exactly, but it was very good, we shall have to wait and see..." was her reply.

Week after week after week, I prayed and pleaded that we had won the food in the picture. Eventually, as time rolled on, I began to realise that if we had won the people would have let us know by now. I also became doubtful as to whether or not Mum had even sent it in. I asked Eve what she thought – she just shrugged and said, "Don't know."

That night Eve went up to bed before me. When I entered the bedroom she was sitting on the bed in her nightclothes. She looked like a deer caught in headlights: wide-eyed and shaking. She was staring, unmoving. I asked her what was wrong and she slowly lifted her arm and pointed at the wardrobe; she opened her mouth but did not speak.

I could see nothing unusual so sat on the bed beside her. As I put my arm around her she seemed to snap out of her paralysis and pointed again with vigour. "Look Sue!! Look! Can't you see it?!" she screeched. I looked again; there was a pile of junk in front of the wardrobe. I wondered if there was something I was missing so I jumped off the bed and had a closer look. Eve raised her hands to her face, watching me through her fingers. By this point her fear was beginning to rub off on me, and I half expected something to leap out of the pile and attack me.

There was a screwed up carrier bag on top of some old clothes. As I bent down to pick it up and look under it, Eve let out an almighty scream. I jumped out of my skin, looking all around in panic, but still could not see what had made her so frightened. It seemed to be the bag that was scaring her, so I picked it up and held it out to show her. "Eve, *silly billy* – it's only a bag! You scared me half to death over a bag!" The fear had subsided and I found myself giggling at my foolishness. It really is amazing how fear can be contagious even when the cause of it is unknown. But there was no calming Eve down. She continued to shake and began to sob. Between giggles I tried to reassure her; we got into bed, and eventually she calmed down and we both fell asleep.

I have since learned that Spirit can make people see what they want them to. I saw nothing but an ordinary carrier bag, but Eve saw a wild cat upon the pile of clothes, snarling and poised to attack. I felt sorry that Eve only ever seemed to be affected by negative Spirit.

At least I often had Good Spirits to protect and calm me and show me nice things. On cold nights we used to boil a kettle up on the greasy gas stove in the kitchen to make our hot water bottles. These were glass lemonade bottles, with thick glass bases. We never had rubber hot water bottles like our friends did. Thinking back it was rather dangerous, although Dad always said, "Make sure you have enough cold water in the bottom first," inevitably we had nights where the glass would crack from the heat. This resulted in boiling water and glass spitting out at whoever was making their bottle, and unless there was another glass pop bottle to be had you went cold that night. We rarely had pop so it could be some while before you got another bottle, unless we managed to retrieve one from someone else's rubbish.

Once in bed and feeling warm enough, I would take my bottle from under the covers and peer into the glass base, which acted as a crystal ball. I stared at the glass for a while, even though a glass bottle full of water can get heavy very quickly. I kept asking to see something nice and pretty, something to make me feel happy. Slowly but surely things would appear. I saw beautiful and graceful fairies, all with different coloured dresses, busily dancing round in the bottom of the glass. They were then followed by the energetic, lively ballet dancers putting on a show. Next, it would be a multi-coloured merry-go-round from a fairground. It was better than watching television, and indeed I felt calmer and happier and able to drift off to sleep.

It was October 1969, and bonfire night was fast approaching. It was a major annual event for us, as all the children down the street made their own bonfires in the field. It was a competition, and a matter of pride to have the biggest, most impressive fire. Our bonfire stood about ten feet tall and we still had a couple of days left to add to it. We were determined to make this year's the best ever and were working together, and having great fun in the process. We were all trying to find dead branches in the field and swamp area.

We split up, each looking for the choicest dead wood. I wandered off alone and came across a whole tree that had fallen the previous winter. I called to Joe excitedly to come and help me – what a fantastic find! As I turned around impatiently to see if he had heard me I was shocked to see a lady standing right in front of my face.

She looked to be in her mid-twenties with long, dark hair, and she glared at me with a very stern expression. "What ARE you doing?" she demanded. I did not recognise her, but her voice commanded such authority that I felt as though I had to answer her. I told her I was collecting wood for our bonfire. She looked horrified and shouted at me, "It is BAD, BAD to make a fire!" She turned and pointed toward our bonfire. A sick feeling of dread rose within me and my stomach felt as though it had hit the floor.

I followed her finger and looked at the bonfire. "LOOK! LOOK WHAT YOU DID!" she shouted. I saw a lady with a rope around her neck tied to the bonfire, whilst a baying crowd watched and jeered. A man approached the bonfire with a lit torch and proceeded to set fire to the pile of dead wood. A huge cheer rose from the crowd of spectators as the fire ignited, and a sickening crackling sound began as the flames hungrily devoured the bonfire.

I could hear the woman screaming: a desperate, agonised wail that cut through the autumn air. I screamed and ran away, trying to cover my ears and eyes. I did not want to look at the fire, but because I was not looking where I was going I tripped over. When I looked up I saw that the lady with the dark hair had been following me. Her eyes looked softer now, and she looked at me with compassion. She held out her hand and helped me up. When I had regained my balance she was looking at me intensely. "I'm sorry," she said in softer tones, "I did not realise you were me." This made no sense, and only served to terrify me further, so, without looking back, I ran home as fast as my legs could carry me.

After a few moments I calmed down and ventured a look from the bedroom window overlooking where our bonfire had been. My guide Michael was by my side: he reassured me there was nothing that could hurt me, it was only Spirit showing me a past life, and I was safe. The bonfire was still there, just a pile of benevolent twigs and bracken; it had not been lit and there was no one around. I sat on Mum's bed for a long while. I closed my eyes and asked in my mind that I not be shown that sort of thing again. Next thing I realised, Dad was standing next to me, looking worried. Joe had told him that he saw me running home scared and looking a funny colour.

"What's the matter Susan, are you feeling bad?" Dad asked.

"Oh no, I just saw something horrible," I said, still shaking.

"What was it, a snake?" shouted Joe.

"No, no, it was a lady on top of the bonfire, her clothes were burning and she was screaming," I sobbed.

"Like a witch!" Joe squealed. "You seen a witch!"

With that, Dad got hold of my arm and said, "That's it young lady, I've had enough of this silly talk. You're beginning to scare everyone."

He was very angry. "You go to your room now, no more playing for you today! I tell you I'm taking you to church on Sunday and see if we can't sort you out!"

I was still crying when Dad slammed the bedroom door after telling me I'd be going to bed without any dinner that night. I thought, 'What's new?'

Dad did take me to church the following Sunday. At one point I saw him talking to Father O'Toole, but nothing seemed to come of it.

However, a few weeks later, one Saturday afternoon, two of Dad's cousins, who were both nuns, came and took us out. When I heard they were coming I thought it may be because Dad told them how angry I'd made him about the lady on the bonfire. I said to Dad, "What do we call 'em, them being nuns?"

"They are just your Aunty Ena and Aunty Alice, that's all Susan. No need to be afraid: they are normal people," Dad replied.

They took all of us to Windsor, and we went to a posh tearoom. It was wonderful, all manner of fancy cakes, crumpets and fruit loafs were there for us to eat! I whispered to Dad that this was, "Not normal!" We had a great time and the nuns laughed and smiled a lot. After the tea room we all took a stroll along the Thames – Aunty Ena was walking alongside me and we gradually fell back from the rest of the family. She said she knew about the things I saw. I was horrified: I really thought she was going to damn me to hell. But she smiled kindly and said, "Between you and me I see things too – but we must never tell other people. It may frighten them because they won't understand."

Just after Christmas, I remember waking up in the early hours of the morning when everyone else was fast asleep. I needed to go to the toilet, but tried hard to ignore the nagging pain in my bladder. Getting up in the night was something I did not like to do as I knew that the not-so-nice Spirit in the loft would try to scare me. So, I rolled over, closed my eyes, and tried to convince myself that I did not need to go. I soon realised it was futile. I could lay there in discomfort, unable to sleep, or I could brave it, rush there and back and hopefully get some sleep.

I glanced over at Eve, who was sleeping soundly. For a split second I contemplated waking her and asking her to come with me. I decided against it: not because she would think me silly or mad, but because she would be more scared than I was if I told her the reason for my apprehension.

I got out of bed and lingered at the bedroom door for a full minute or two. My eyes searched the darkness of the landing for anything untoward, and I held my breath to better listen to the night. Eventually I decided that the coast was as clear as it would ever be. I stepped out of the bedroom and bolted across the landing to the toilet on tip-toes, so as not to wake the others.

I sat on the toilet leaning forward with the door slightly ajar unable to take my eyes off the landing even for a second. I felt as though if I turned away or let my guard down something in the darkness would get me. Suddenly, I saw a thick mist beginning to descend from the ceiling. It seemed to be seeping from the hatch that led to the loft. As I watched it coiled and thickened until I could no longer see my way back to the bedroom. As it came closer it seemed to emit a chill, and goose bumps rose on my arms. Suddenly I could see my breath in the air and I began to shiver.

I was scared and asked Michael to come to me. I waited as the mist grew thicker and the air turned colder, but I couldn't see him, or even feel him around. All I could feel was the chill of the mist, and all I could sense was darkness and fear. I took a deep breath and ran through the mist in the direction of my bedroom, and, fumbling, I found the door and managed to get through it and shut it behind me. I did not look back. Eve stirred but did not waken as, with my heart pounding, I got into bed and pulled the covers around me. I sat watching the door for a while, worried that the mist would begin to creep in under the door. Eventually I fell asleep, and when I woke in the morning the mist was gone.

It was January 1970 when I realised I was often going to be shown past lives I had lived. My first one, as Michael had explained, was the lady I saw just before bonfire night last year.

In February 1970 I began having recurring dreams. I say dreams but actually, although I believed them to be so, Michael eventually told me I was being shown a particular vision of one of my past lives. He said the lady I saw was me. After this dream had recurred five or six times, the same scenario was played before my eyes in the daytime, when I was obviously awake and certainly not dreaming.

The lady was in a long brown dress and heavily pregnant. She walked what seemed miles carrying a little girl about two years old. She walked through a wooded area, but seemed unsure which way to go. She stopped briefly, sitting to rest on a fallen tree trunk. The child she had been carrying was very quiet and seemed to almost be in a trance. She eventually scooped her back up, and carried on walking through overgrown brambles and monstrous tree roots. When she reached the edge of the wood she stepped out into the sunshine, fell into the sweet soft grass that lay all around her and slept cuddling the child.

Some while after, she woke with twinges in her abdomen; she knew she must move on and find shelter. She struggled to her feet, and the young child put her arms up to be carried again. The vision of the child at this point made it apparent that it was so frail it was certainly not able to walk by itself.

The lady kept going through the night; the full moon picking her out as she struggled across the rough countryside. Just as the sun began to peer over the horizon she saw a barn a way off and headed for that.

With only 30 minutes to spare before the birth, she laid down in the soft hay and the seclusion of this barn. There were no signs of other buildings or farms around, not even any livestock.

She gave birth to a boy, with the little girl looking on in absolute bewilderment. She managed to cut the cord with a rough, sharp implement carried on her belt. The new-born baby rolled from her into the hay as she began to haemorrhage uncontrollably. She died within ten minutes in a massive pool of blood.

The baby boy died a couple days later, cradled in the little girl's arms. She died a few days after that. I really wanted to know more about why this had happened, but to this day it has not been explained to me.

Another past life I was shown at this time was, yet again, a vision and not a dream. Michael told me as soon as I began to visualise this that it was a past life of mine. I felt I was living in America; my husband had two other wives, and we all lived together, with lots of children, in a log cabin in the woods. We did not seem to be in contact with any other people.

We washed ourselves in a fast flowing stream at the bottom end of the cabin's garden. The three of us would do all the clothes washing in the stream as well. I seemed to be very tired and weak, but carried on with the chores anyway.

The next time I was shown this life I was in bed with a fever; I could see the beads of sweat on my brow and the red flush of my skin. I was coughing badly.

The final time I saw the vision was a few weeks later. I was being buried on top of a hill with all my extended family present.

CHAPTER 5

I was playing in the middle of the Pit with my younger brother Andy who was by now almost seven years old. The Pit was what all the local kids called the vast area of land behind all our council houses. In fact you could see to the other side of the deep excavated area to more council houses – all the same, but by gosh a wonderful post-war victory in council management on the edge of an also vast and growing trading estate.

Andy and I were sitting down pretending to make some tea. My stomach made a gurgling noise; I was very hungry and was pretending we had jam doughnuts to eat. I was remembering once, a while back, when Dad took us to the Spot Café in Slough Market, and he bought us all a cup of tea and a jam doughnut – a memorable treat indeed. Sally our little dog was wandering around us; she was a love and really enjoyed playing with us kids. She followed us all over the fields, the Swamp, and the Pit all day and half of the evening until we were all called in for tea before bed.

Sally suddenly started growling. When I looked up (from my 'doughnut') to see what the problem was, I saw two boys about my age and a little girl of about three. They all looked dishevelled, dirty and, even by our standards, scruffy kids. Even though I was only ten years old myself, I felt their clothes were from a different time, very old fashioned and they reminded me of some I saw in a book at the school library.

They came and sat down with us, and the little girl held out her hand and asked, "Tea, tea peas?" I pretended to pour a cup of tea into her hand; she looked sideways at me and smiled, her large brown eyes sparkling, and she pretended to drink it. "Thank you," she said.

One of the boys, who could have been twins, (the one on the right) said, "Do ya wanna come and find snakes wiv us?"

Andy and I jumped up and said, "Yeah," and we all went over to the Snake Pit: a different area between the field and Swamp that had lots of blackberry bushes, and where all the kids thought most snakes hid at the bottom.

We played with the 'Twins' and the little girl for about an hour. They said they were from London. When they said they had to go home, I immediately asked if they would like to come back to our house. When they declined I asked if they would come back to play the next day. They nodded and walked away, whilst Andy and I just stood and watched them disappear into the distance – not once did they look back.

The next day I hung about the Snake Pit all day but they never showed. It was some weeks afterwards when I realised that if they were Spirit, Andy had seen and played with them too. This became strikingly obvious when one day something happened that Dad, although in the same room, was totally unaware of.

The living room in our house was the only room which had any heating. On cold days we would all vie for a place in front of its coal fire. One particularly chilly April day Dad and I were sat by the fire, keeping warm, when I heard a knock on the living room door. "Come in," I said, but no one did so I got up and opened the door.

As I did I felt a freezing, forceful wind blow right through me. I stepped back involuntarily, and could see a thick black fog seeping into the room. "Dad!" I cried. "Look!"

He glanced up from his paper at the open doorway and then at me. "What?" he said. I knew then that he couldn't see the coiling, black substance that was slowly filling the room from the floor upwards.

"Oh, nothing, my mistake," I replied, remembering Aunty Ena's advice, and he carried on reading. It was surreal to see him sat there, totally oblivious, as first his ankles and then his knees were shrouded in the fog.

I told myself to ignore it, and sat down next to Dad. Our dog Sally had begun to growl quietly, and I could see her fur standing on end and her back arched. Almost immediately a huge black spider came flying at me, as though it had been thrown, and landed in my lap. I shot up out of my seat, screaming (I never have been able to tolerate spiders). "Stop it! Stop it! Go away!" I shouted. Dad thought I was screaming at the spider (which, to be fair, is my normal reaction to the eight legged monsters), but I was actually shouting at the negative Spirit that was trying to frighten me.

Dad just tutted. "No use shouting at it, love," he said.

I looked round and couldn't see where the spider had gone because of the black fog around my legs. Sally was whimpering and I was fearful the spider would fly at me again, so I scooped Sally up in my arms and ran upstairs to my bedroom with her. I stayed in my bedroom all afternoon playing and sewing buttons on my old school dress. Dad would shout up from time to time saying things like, "Silly Sue scared of a baby spider, come down and have a cuppa tea love, the spider's long gone." Dad didn't know it was not the spider I was really scared of.

I could not explain to Dad what I was feeling and experiencing: unlike Andy, he had no idea of the spirit world. I so loved him, and he was trying in the best way he knew to make me feel wanted, grown up, and an important part of the family. This may, in part, have been because of the way Mum treated me. Dad made me responsible for certain things, like making sure Andy crossed the road safely on the way to school.

I remember one morning I was feeling very hungry. I was taking Andy over the field to see him across the road. He was playing and ran on ahead of me. I felt so tired and weak I could not catch up with him. I tried to shout at him not to cross the road before I got there, but nothing came out of my mouth – I could see he was laughing. Next minute, I realised he was already on the other side of the road, and was waving at me as he continued on to school. I came over as if I was about to faint; I had to sit down in the middle of the field, and I knew I would not make it back home. My vision was blurry, my hands were shaking and my limbs turned to jelly. I had to sit there for about thirty minutes before I felt able to walk slowly back home.

I was also due in school that day, but there was no way I would have made it. Due to lack of food in the house, I had not eaten anything to speak of in about a week. Unfortunately, once you went to secondary school free school meals stopped. I went to lie on my bed; I drifted off to sleep, but was woken by Michael calling to me, telling me to drink some water. His voice seemed far away and very quiet, but he kept on and on telling me over and over again to drink some water; he just would not let me sleep. After a while I could not stand it any longer; I pulled myself up and into the bathroom and drank some. He told me to drink more; I did, and although I felt sick, I kept drinking until I really could not take another drop. Michael said, "OK you can stop now." The pains in my stomach were so awful I had to go and lay down again.

Dad came in later, and I told him I was not well enough to go to school. He told me to stay in bed until I felt better, and at tea time he brought me up a cup of Oxo; it was delicious and I felt much better after that.

I was beginning to think perhaps the lack of food was making me feel bad.

In November, two months after starting at secondary school, I had another vision of myself in a past life. I was living in London and I was about four years old. It looked like we were living in an underground tunnel. I was filthy with matted hair and torn dirty clothes. There were lots of rats running around my bare feet. My Mum looked just as dirty and awful. I had difficulty with my breathing, and saw myself deteriorating. I was sweating, shaking and coughing. The rain was coming in under the tunnel. I was a sorry state and actually watched myself drift off and die.

Michael continued to let me know whether the visions I had were of past lives or premonitions. I have to say that, in all the past lives I have been shown, I am female with long, dark brown hair and dark brown eyes. Having said this, I feel past lives can be lived as male or female.

One of the visions I had was as an eighteen-year-old gypsy girl with long, brown, curly hair. I was a traveller, as were all my family, and we were always on the move.

All the young men liked me: I was particularly attractive in this life, very vibrant and playful, sexy but wilful. In the vision, I was running away from a man: I was crossing a small stream, splashing and lifting my skirts as I went. He caught up with me; picked me up in his strong arms, carried me to his wagon and threw me aboard it. Then he jumped on the back too and gave me such a hug. We seemed madly in love with each other and happy beyond belief. Michael told me this was a long, long time ago, but was one of my happiest lives, to date.

One morning I woke at 5am, and I just could not get back off to sleep. I had an uneasy feeling in my stomach that I could not explain. I had school in the morning and was getting a little agitated with myself, for having the inability to settle. I switched the light on and decided to read a little in the hope this would do the trick and get me back off to sleep again. I could not get into the book either, so just lay there thinking, when all of a sudden I was no longer in my room. It seemed as if I was watching a television. I was at a lake that I recognised as Virginia Water. Some years before this we had visited Virginia Water with my Dad's Aunty Ethel, who lived nearby. We had all walked around the lake after lunch – it was lovely and we actually seemed like any normal family that day.

What happened next, I now know for sure, was a premonition, but it was many years before I realised this.

I was sitting on a bench facing the lake; it was dark, but I could see clearly with the brightness of the moonlight. A dark saloon car pulled up in the car park behind me. The driver got out of the car and opened the boot. A further two men got out of the car and joined him. They were all talking, but I could not hear what they were saying. I somehow knew they could not see me.

They lifted an old rolled-up carpet out of the boot. It appeared very heavy, as all three of them were struggling to carry it. They walked to the nearest edge of the water and put the carpet bundle down on the ground. There seemed to be some disagreement, but eventually they picked up the carpet again and walked further along the water's edge. Once again they stopped, but instead of putting down the bundle they threw it into the dark, cold, unforgiving water. One man stayed and watched as the bundle slowly sank, the other two had practically run back to the car already. The car's engine started, and the third man ran to get in before they sped off.

I asked Michael what it was that I had just been shown. He told me the men had been dumping the body of a night-watchman they had murdered. He said they had killed him because he had foiled a robbery they were undertaking. Then I realised that was why I had had the uneasy feeling in my stomach. I was just as suddenly back in my bed; there was no way I could go to sleep now.

My mind was reeling; I was sure this sort of thing did not happen to many people. Although I trusted Michael with my life, I still could not understand why it was happening to me.

It was not until many years later that I met one of the men who had dumped the body of that poor night-watchman in the lake.

By this time I was working full time as a medium, giving readings to people five or six days a week.

A man called Pete rang up and booked a sitting with me. He asked for a map as he said he came from London and did not know my area very well – he was apparently just staying with friends for a couple of weeks.

When the day of his sitting came I had an uneasy feeling and asked Michael if everything was OK. He told me that Pete had not given me his correct name; that he wasn't a very nice man, but I was in no danger.

Michael always protects me: if it was not going to be good or safe for me he would have told me to cancel.

When Pete arrived for his sitting he seemed very nervous, so I offered him a cup of tea and invited him to sit down. I told him how the process works and told him not to worry. I said what I always say:

"Spirit knows everything; they know everything that has happened and everything that is going to happen to you. They should tell you what you need to know, not necessarily what you want to know."

This was his very first reading, and I guess he was in his late fifties, so I told him they may want to talk for a week, but all we have is an hour so I hope they will give you what they feel is most important.

His father came back, who had died ten years earlier. His Dad was bringing in a 'New' spirit feeling with him, a lady to one side of him. She was a very strong Mum feeling. I asked her who she was, and she gestured towards Pete and said, "His mum, he's my little baby."

I told Pete that I had his mum here and that she had not been gone long.

He nodded and said, "That's right, she only died last week." Then he burst into tears.

I then relayed many messages from her, but only the ones he was able to hear and deal with in his grief at this time. He seemed as happy as anyone could who had lost a lovely mum so recently. A couple of friends and relatives came through at the end of the reading. Pete was very appreciative, and asked me to tell his mum and dad that he loved them. I said I did not need to pass on that message as they were right here and already knew. He said he was very grateful and pleased to know that his mum and dad were together in the Spirit world so soon after her parting.

As he stood to leave, I was shown the premonition I had as a child at Virginia Water. I was a little taken aback, and then his dad said, "My son was the driver."

I told Pete that his dad was showing me a man driving a car, years ago, with two male passengers. They went to Virginia Water. He then showed me a body wrapped in carpet. They took it out of the boot and dumped it in the water.

With that Pete's chin hit the floor and he went very pale. Eventually he asked me why his dad would be showing me that.

I told Pete that I wasn't sure, but that perhaps the men involved were linked to him, so to be careful.

"As I said before Pete they know everything."

CHAPTER 6

Throughout my younger years I had some very frightening negative experiences from Spirit. One of the most terrifying has always stayed with me.

At the bottom of the school playing field, overlooking the children at play, stood an old brick house named 'Fir's Corner'. The house was provided for the school caretaker and his family. As the caretakers at our school never seemed to stay for very long the house was often unoccupied.

In many ways the house was beautiful: it was detached with gardens on all sides and large trees framed the borders; yet it filled me with an eerie unease. When I looked at it my skin prickled and goose bumps forced their way onto my flesh. I was overwhelmed with a sense of nameless foreboding, as though some dark truth waited to reveal itself – hinting its malevolence to me. I did not like to look at it, but to turn my back on the house was to feel as though some unseen evil lurked behind me, its gaze upon me. But the eyes I felt sure were watching me, seemed not to be just looking at my physical self, but deeper, as if into my soul.

One part of the house drew my gaze in particular – a window, beneath the eaves, at the front of the house. I sensed that something unnatural and dark resided behind that glass. On several occasions, when yet another caretaker had abandoned the school and I knew the house was unoccupied, I would glance up at that window just in time to see a figure turn and walk away from it. Were these the eyes I felt upon me?

A new caretaker arrived at the beginning of December, bringing with him his wife and daughter. The girl – Andrea – was put in my class. She was a very timid soul and had an air of innocence about her. She seemed to cling to childhood, and the call of adolescence, which was beginning to touch and change the rest of my peers, had not yet affected her. Whilst the boys and girls in my year seemed compelled to feign what they thought to be maturity – shunning their childhood in the eager pursuit of growing-up – she treasured dolls and childish games above conforming to the crowd. I liked her instantly, and we quickly became friends, preferring each other's company to that of any of the other girls in our class.

It wasn't long before Andrea's mum, obviously delighted that her shy, quiet (and somewhat backward) child had made a friend so quickly and, eager to show support and encouragement, invited me for dinner at Fir's Corner. I felt sick; I had been trying not to think about the fact that my friend lived in the house that filled me with such dread. I couldn't refuse: Andrea was my friend, and the last thing I wanted to do was upset her. Aside from which, I was genuinely concerned for her. I couldn't believe that she could live in such a place and not feel the obvious darkness that was in the air. It seemed to surround the entire house, and when I was near, caused me to have such a dread in my stomach I felt sick.

As we approached the house together after school every fibre of my body screamed at me to turn around, to run and not look back. The fear I felt seemed to make my imagination run wild. It seemed to me that the old, majestic trees that surrounded Fir's Corner were twisted and contorted, as if in terror. The absence of birdsong made the air deafeningly silent, except for the rhythmic rustling of leaves that sounded like urgent whisperings. Stepping through the front door my stomach hit the floor. My heartbeat accelerated, and I could hear my own pulse thundering in my ears. I forced myself to breathe evenly, as I was becoming dizzy, and fought to keep my composure.

Looking around I was struck by how drab and shabby the interior of the house looked. It was almost devoid of furniture and appeared not to have been decorated for many years. Paint was peeling from the skirting boards, which were yellowed with age, and the carpets were frayed and worn. The wallpaper was very old-fashioned, and the air was musty and cloying. Afterwards I thought about this lack of modern, fresh décor, and it dawned on me it was probably that none of the previous caretakers had stayed long enough to do it up.

It was a warm sunny day so Andrea suggested we play in the back garden. I hastily agreed, glad of the opportunity to get out of this strange and disconcerting house. As I stepped out of the back door I felt as though a weight had lifted from me. I was out of that oppressive building and, mercifully, out of sight of the upstairs window that filled me with such apprehension. I began to forget my misgivings as I played with my cherished friend.

After a while Andrea wanted to go and play in her bedroom. Even as we began to ascend the stairs I knew, with absolute certainty, which room she would present to me as her bedroom. My stomach churned and contracted, my throat felt tight and I had difficulty swallowing. I was close to being paralysed with terror, but somehow I lifted one leaden foot after the other and followed her to the front bedroom I feared so much.

Whenever I recall what happened next my mind's eye views it in black and white, as if watching an old movie. This may in part be due to the stark appearance of the room itself. As Andrea opened the door and we stepped in I saw that the room was completely bare except for her bed, on which a solitary ragged doll sat slumped – its eyes on the door. There were thick dark curtains at the window.

Just then Andrea's mum called up to her, wanting to see her about something downstairs. Andrea rolled her eyes, told me she would be right back, and raced off to see her mother. I was alone, in the room behind the window.

The temperature in the room plummeted. Cold sticky sweat began to coat my skin, and sickening, prickly shivers raced up my spine like spiders scuttling up a drainpipe. A cold breeze blew hard across my face and the door slammed shut. As I reached for the doorknob I already knew that the door would not open. It felt as though there were some resistance on the other side, a force much stronger pulling against me.

Suddenly, the stuck door ceased to be my primary concern as I became aware of someone behind me. Shaking from head to foot, panic washing over me in waves that made me dizzy and threatened to knock me off my feet, I turned around slowly.

The sorry looking doll was no longer alone on the bed. A teenage girl (who looked to be just a few years older than me) sat beside it, and her dark, sunken eyes, set deep into unnaturally pale skin, glared at me. Dark straggled hair framed her face; her gaze was unwavering.

"Who are you?" I managed to ask with a whisper.

"This is MY room," the girl shouted. "I don't want you or Andrea in here!" Still her eyes did not look away from mine.

"Why?" I asked.

"You do not belong here, so you should go," came the hostile reply.

Still shaking, I explained to her that I was unable to open the door. Suddenly, it flew open with such force that it slammed back against the wall. The girl jumped up from the bed as if in fright and looked out of the window. When she turned to face me again the steely hostility in her expression was replaced by panic. Her eyes had widened and she seemed all at once to be a scared child, not the threatening vision I had at first thought her to be. She began to walk towards me and gestured to the door.

"GO! GO NOW!! Before my uncle hurts you!" she urged, and the fear and sadness behind her eyes were overwhelming. My stomach knotted, and I felt tears welling up inside me, although I did not know the reason for this grief.

As she turned her head to check out of the window again, I saw blood pouring from her neck. "Ar...Are you alright?" I stammered.

She did not look at me. "HE did it," she said simply. There were footsteps climbing the stairs, and she vanished right before my eyes just as Andrea walked back into the bedroom.

"Did you see her?!" I asked Andrea urgently. "Did you see that girl?" Andrea shook her head, and seeing that I was obviously shaken by something, put her arm around me. When my panic had passed we talked at length, and Andrea confessed that she had been having nightmares: terrible, violent and disturbing nightmares, ever since they had moved to Fir's Corner.

As she recounted her dreams we both felt the terrible chill invade the room again. The curtains whipped up into the air as if caught by a sudden gale and blew towards us, totally horizontal, at a height above our heads. It was as if a storm raged and the windows were open – they were not.

As we faced each other, frozen with fear, we heard Andrea's mother, who was oblivious to what was happening upstairs in her house, shout for us to come down for tea.

Andrea snatched up her rag doll from the bed, and with the curtains still blowing wildly we bolted downstairs as fast as we could. Andrea never said a word to her mum about what had just happened.

I ate my dinner so quickly that I was left with a terrible ache of indigestion, made an excuse about my mother needing me home to help with my younger brother, and left that house as fast as I could – never to set foot in it again.

A couple of months later Andrea told me that they were moving again. Her mum, she said, did not like the house so her dad had found work elsewhere. I was desperately sorry to be losing my friend, but I also felt relieved. I did not like to think of her living in that house, and in that room.

Over the years I have often thought about the girl in that room. Did she ever meet another person with the ability to talk to her? Did she manage to get the help she desperately needed? Or was I, who was not mature or developed enough to deal with her pain, the only one who ever came to her? I know now that the fear and foreboding I felt about Fir's Corner came from her, from her terror and the echoes of the terrible violence that occurred there. Did she ever find peace?

After Andrea moved away I felt lonely for a while, apart from my Spirit friends. But it was not long before a group of girls in my class started to include me more and more in their chats and games, and I soon felt I belonged.

Having said this, I found I had lots of fun with Joe and his best friend at the time, Dave, especially during the summer holidays. One day Joe, Dave and I decided to go and wander around the trading estate. We particularly enjoyed standing at the back of the local chocolate and sweet factory – smelling the odour of hundreds of different sweets being made was lovely.

We watched a man who appeared from a small blue door at the back of the factory. He had a large tin drum in his hands. As we spied on what he did we saw him walk to a skip, and, to our astonishment, he tipped loads of chocolate and sweets into it from the drum. We could not believe our eyes!

When he went back through the blue door, we sat down and made a plan. We decided to wait till dark, and then the boys could climb over the fence with a carrier bag, get into the skip and pinch all the sweets they could carry. I was to be lookout.

Once dusk arrived the boys scaled the fence, ran to the skip and hid behind it to make sure the coast was clear. All was quiet, and Joe, who was more nimble and of a lesser build than Dave, scrambled into the skip. He was passing out lumps of sweets and chocolates to Dave who was putting them into the bag we had found in a nearby bin. Then to our horror we heard a door slam. Although it was some way off in the factory it panicked all of us. Joe jumped out of the skip and both he and Dave ran towards me. Dave chucked the bag over the fence to me and shouted, "RUN!!"

My legs felt like jelly, and my breathing was rapid, but shallow, but by God did I run. I left the boys still clambering over the fence. I was away. Eventually they caught up with me but none of us stopped until we reached the field near our house.

We flopped down in the grass once we felt we were safe from being caught. After getting our breath back Dave shared out all the sweets three ways. I could not believe my eyes, I had a slab of chocolate the size of a dinner plate and a congealed chunk of chewy fruits the size of a side plate, plus various bits and bobs of well-known but deformed chocolate bars.

I ate and ate and ate until I was actually sick, vomiting multi-colours, but hey, it was good.

We decided we had better go home: it was rather late. I hid my remaining sweets behind my back as we went in. When I got upstairs I woke Andy up for a midnight feast – but only if he swore not to tell. He loved it.

Later that night I felt a bit guilty. I knew it was wrong to steal, but I justified it in my head by thinking I was very, very hungry and anyway the factory was only going to throw it away.

All three of us went back to that factory a few more times, but eventually we were caught. Ironically it was on an evening when the skip was empty. The boys got away but the man from the factory caught me by the arm as I ran. He shook me hard and shouted, "Why are you stealing!" I was speechless and frightened. The boys came back and threw a few stones at him and he let me go, but shouted after us. "If I ever see you here again the police will take you to jail."

We never returned, but it was good for a while to have an endless supply of sweets.

One Saturday morning, later in the holidays, I went to play with my friend Jane and her elder sister Helen. They lived across the Pit from our house. I think their mum had died, but I never liked to ask them where she was, they just never had one.

Their dad was nice, if a little overpowering: a little loud. He used to call me Susie Ping Pong, I did not know why, but I did know it annoyed me. Anyhow, this particular Saturday he asked me if I would like to go down town with them as they were all going shopping.

I ran home to ask if I was allowed to go with them. Dad said yes, and he even gave me twenty pence to pay for the bus and buy a sweet. I ran back to their house so excited. We got the bus down town. The High Street was packed and Jane and I held hands so we did not get lost. Helen and her dad held hands and walked in front of us. We went into the Market Place and Pets' Corner had little kittens and puppies for sale. They were adorable; I especially loved the soft puppies clambering at the cage to get my attention. One licked my hand and wagged his tail so fast I thought it would snap off. The lady selling them came over to me; she seemed lovely and asked me in a gentle voice if I wanted a puppy. I told her I would love to but I already had a sweet dog called Sally and my mum would go mad if I took one home. She said kindly, "Never mind. See if you can and come back next week, I expect they will still be here then." I nodded, but I knew it would be a cold day in hell the day Mum would let me have a puppy. Apart from the fact it would be something I could love and would love me back, she was always complaining about Sally, the dog we already had.

We all started to walk away when I felt the urge to run back and give her a message I was getting. I squeezed her hand

and said, "Your mum says Danny is going to die tonight, be with him."

The lady slapped her hand to her mouth in shock, and then she said "How... How do you know he is ill?"

I just said, "He will be fine; your mum is coming to be with him."

I ran back to Helen and Jane. Their dad took us into Spot Café and bought us all a coca cola and a biscuit: what a lovely treat.

The lady from Pets' Corner kept looking over to me in the café. All I could do was smile at her. It made me wonder why I saw things about other people, their lives and deaths. I still did not understand what was really happening. Sometimes I saw bad things, sometimes lovely things. The feeling I had about the pet shop lady was a calm and peaceful feeling – her mum wanted her to know things would be OK.

I continued to have visions of my past lives. In one of these I was living in Scotland. I lived in a big, secluded house with high walls all around. It must, I believe, have been a very important man I was married to. The home was massive, we had servants, and I had everything I could want in the way of clothes and jewellery etc. But I did not have my freedom.

The man I was married to was a dominant, obsessive and malicious misogynist. He made me call him Master as he did the servants. I could not even invite girlfriends to tea to talk about home-making or cooking skills etc. I was, to all intents and purposes, a prisoner.

Before we married he was Mr Charming, but now, after several years of violent physical and mental abuse, I kept trying to escape. I think he began to realise I would continue until I succeeded.

The last time I tried I very nearly made it, but he caught me. His anger consumed him and he grabbed at my throat with both hands whilst shaking my head backwards and forwards. He strangled me, and then afterwards put me naked into a deep bath. He told the servants I had fainted in the bath and drowned. No one questioned it – no one ever questioned The Master. I went back over the next few years, in Spirit, to try to warn off other women he was interested in marrying. I hoped to prevent other women ending up as I did.

CHAPTER 7

My friends Teresa and Breda, who lived opposite us in Chiltern Drive, must have told their mum that I talked to Spirit because one day she wanted me to do a reading for her. She was known to all the kids down the street as Aunty Mary: a lovely, short lady with a thick Irish accent. She was a devout Catholic, but, unlike my dad, was also a strong believer in the Spirit world.

Although initially I was unsure as to what she expected from me, and somewhat worried that Dad would find out, I went with my friends to their house. When I saw her she asked me if I could see any dead people around her.

I said, "Yes, I can. I can see lots of people, but it is your mum that stands out."

She began to cry and she said, "I was sure you would do, Susan." Then she asked me to go and sit down with her.

Once seated in the living room she said, "Has she got any messages for me, Susan?"

"She says you haven't lost your glasses, they are in Roger's jacket pocket hanging up in the outhouse. She's also giving you a bunch of large daisies."

At this Aunty Mary sobbed again. "They were her favourite flowers." She cried, "Is Mum alright where she is?"

"She's fine, her foot doesn't hurt anymore, and she doesn't miss you because she sees you every day and wants you to keep your chin up and be happy," I told her. "She says thanks for putting her photo out again, she likes it where you can see it."

She was now sobbing uncontrollably. She grabbed me and put her arms round me, cuddling me very hard. "Thank you, thank you so much."

I felt rather embarrassed and awkward and just said, "Well I must go home now." Before I could get out of her house she managed to push thirty pence into my hand.

I thanked her – I could not believe someone was giving me money for what I said; after all, it just made her cry.

A couple of weeks later, Aunty Mary came over and asked if I could come over to her house again; she had something she wanted to ask me. It was only a couple of weeks until Christmas. The sky was dark, and there was heavy rain and a strong icy wind blowing. I chucked on my brown anorak, rather apprehensively, and went across the road to her house. She took me into their living room and we sat down. Teresa and Breda were there as well.

"I was talking to Bernadette the other afternoon, and I told her about the reading you gave me Susan," Aunty Mary said.

"Right."

"Well, Bernadette says can you do one for her. She will come here so you don't have to go all the way to her house," she continued.

"Well, er yes, I don't mind if she wants to," I said.

"She'll pay you Susan, she'll pay you."

"Oh ok, yeah," I replied.

Bernadette was Aunty Mary's younger sister; we knew her as Aunty Bernie as she was a regular and vibrant visitor to their house. She was a pretty lady, with green eyes and black hair that she wore in a beehive.

I went over to Aunty Mary's house later that week as arranged. When I got there Aunty Mary said, "You and Bernadette go in the living room Susan, we'll stay in the kitchen until you're done." As she gestured to Teresa and Breda, my friends smiled at me.

Teresa said, "When you finished I got something in me bedroom I wanna show ya."

When Aunty Bernie and I sat down, she asked if I had anyone special there for her. As soon as she had said this I saw a man standing behind her; he was younger than my dad and was wearing a smart suit. He smiled directly at me but didn't say anything. I described the man to her, and she said, "Yeah, go on, go on, what is he saying?"

I asked him what he wanted to say, and he just handed a red rose to me to give to her. I told her what he had done, and she stared at me in expectation.

He then looked sad, and said, "Sorry."

A tear ran down her face as he said, "I didn't mean to do it. I wanted to marry you and make you happy. I had too much beer and just fell in. I didn't really know anything much about it, only that my clothes were wet," he continued, "I'm so sorry love, but I will wait for you."

He then told her to move on and marry her new man. He didn't mind; he just wanted her to be happy.

We sat silently for a few moments, and then Aunty Bernie said, "Thank you Susan, very much." She gave me thirty pence she had ready on the little table beside her.

"Ooh, thanks very much Aunty Bernie," I said.

"How do you do it Susan? You are very accurate. Do you see lots of Spirits at once, like is everyone there?" she enquired.

"I don't really know, the right Spirit seems to come for the right person and just talk to me," I said. "I can't make anyone come back, and I can't stop anyone coming through either: it's up to them."

"How about 'out of body' experiences. Have you ever had that?"

"I don't understand what you mean by that; hold on, I'll ask Michael. Yes: he says yes and is showing me a dream I've had, which must be out of body; yes he's putting his thumb up to that." I paused and thought about these experiences that I had believed were just vivid dreams, then said to Aunty Bernie, "Yes, definitely, I do have them."

"Well, thanks again Susan, maybe I'll have another reading sometime," Aunty Bernie said.

"Yeah, just let me know if you want one," I replied, and went up to Teresa's bedroom to see what she had to show me.

Looking back, it was around this time, at the age of twelve, I had many out of body experiences. They were very frequent, and very calming.

They always happened when I was asleep, which I suppose is why I used to think they were just dreams. Michael would come to me whilst I slept. He would hold my hand and we would float down the stairs and out of the house without opening the door. I would always be back by morning.

Usually we only floated a few feet from the ground, so that we could see everything; it was great, like flying, but slowly. Occasionally, when necessary, we would go higher above things, to take the whole scene in, like a camera panning out.

One particular night Michael took me down town. We flew over the Adelphi Cinema – I was amazed at all the things on top of the roof. There were skylights, funnel shaped apparatus, wires and poles, birds' nests, and something that looked like a small shed. There was something else that looked like a trap door and lots of litter. I remember it with wonder because from the street the cinema did not give any of these secrets away. We carried on passed the ABC café on the corner of the High Street down the main shopping road, past the Green Shield Stamps shop where you could exchange your hard earned stamps for gifts and gadgets 'essential for today's housewife'. We eventually came to the Golden Lion Public House, situated about halfway down the High Street. We seemed to hover over the pub for a while watching people coming out, laughing or talking loudly. It had started to drizzle and a lady came out putting her umbrella up and then clinging onto the arm of the man she was with as they hurried down the road.

Then I heard a familiar voice, it was Mum. She was chatting and laughing with two African men as they all left the pub together. She squealed at the rain and both men, with Mum in the middle of them, lifted up their jackets to protect her newly permed hairdo. I looked at Michael, he returned the gaze with a very sorrowful look indeed. We flew back home, travelling over Mum's head and the heads of the African men as we went; I tried to call out to her but could not speak. I remember thinking what a very strange dream that was!

Another time we were flying at low level over the swamp area at the bottom of the field. It had started to snow, and the snow was lying on the ground. I was quite excited: I loved snow. I saw a snake just lying on top of the snow, close to the edge of the water. It was a grass snake; I had seen many before, but not in winter as they hibernate. It was very still and, I thought, possibly dead. I tried to reach out and pick it up but could not. Michael took me across the watercress beds behind Breda and Teresa's house, and I saw Aunty Mary looking out of the back bedroom window at the snow. Then I went back to bed.

The next morning I called to Andy as soon as I awoke to see if he wanted to go play in the snow. We headed straight for the area of the swamp I had been the night before with Michael. Sure enough, the snake was still there. It looked, and felt, frozen stiff. I took it home, but Dad did not like the idea of a snake in the house and told me to get rid of it. I wanted to keep it, so I took it out into the back garden. I didn't know whether it was dead or alive, but I found a box to put it in. Then I covered it with some straw we had for our rabbit, so at least it would be warm, if it were not already dead.

I named him Sammy and I put the box in the shed. I checked the box several times that day and, sure enough, about tea time he was starting to move around the box. I was delighted. The next day I made him a more elaborate home, behind the shed. Each day I took him some food and gave him a cuddle. On the third day I went to take him some food, Michael was leaning against the shed with his arms folded (something he often does when he is a little annoyed with me). As I approached he shook his head at me. I just said, "What?"

He told me that I would have to let Sammy go: that it was not fair to keep him in a box; that he was not getting the right food, and that he should be hibernating now.

"If you keep him in there he will not survive."

"I thought I was doing a good job. What should I give him to eat then?" I asked.

Michael just raised his voice and said, "Let him go!" and vanished before my eyes.

I could only say "But…" as I opened the box to feed him I could tell Sammy was desperately trying to get out.

I picked him up and took him in the house so that Andy could say goodbye to him. I took him down to the place near the swamp where I had found him. At least the snow had cleared, and I felt sure he would nestle comfortably under some log or reeds to hibernate. I kissed him and let him go, and with tears in my eyes I headed home. Teresa was outside her front gate and noticed I was crying. She said, "I've been looking for you Susan, what's the matter?"

"I've had to let Sammy, my snake, go back into the wild, it's just upset me a bit."

Teresa was a good friend, and we sat talking on her doorstep for some while. She said Sammy would be better off in the wild, it would be more natural for him.

After a while talking with her I felt a bit better and asked her what she had wanted me for. She wanted to know if I had ever used an Ouija board. I said no, but we could make one. Teresa and her sister, Breda, were fascinated with the idea of Spirits and the occult (as many teenage girls are at some stage). This was especially so since I had given readings to both their mum and their aunty already.

Together we made an Ouija board with letters written on cardboard from an empty box we found over by the watercress beds behind their house. It was a crude design, but Spirit are not interested in bells and whistles, so it was perfectly serviceable for three girls wishing to play an exciting game with the unknown. I knew I could see Spirit and didn't need to get messages this way, but it was a bit of fun and my friends thought it was great. I think I enjoyed it all the more because it was a way of sharing my secret life with them.

I was careful to keep the board a secret. I knew that Dad would go mad if he knew (believing such things to be the toys of the devil). I was also aware of how scared Eve was of such things, so it was important to me to ensure that she never found out – not because she would tell (she wouldn't), but because she would not sleep if she knew. If I ever played in our house, alone or with friends, I made sure no one was around. As long as Dad was down the bookies and the coast was clear I would use it on the Formica table in the kitchen.

I kept the homemade Ouija letters in a glass in a hidden place at the back of the cupboard on the kitchen wall. Sometimes when I walked into the room I could hear the letters rattle impatiently, as if to tell me that someone wanted to talk to me. Fortunately, no one else in the family appeared to hear them, so my secret was safe. Often the glass would begin to move on its own even before I had finished setting the board up.

One afternoon, when everyone was out, I was sat at the table playing Ouija alone. Mum came home unexpectedly. She had been out shopping with Aunty Pat, but they had had a row so she walked off. As soon as she came into the kitchen she saw at once what I was doing. Her expression changed rapidly from surprise to anger, and she shouted, "What are you up to??

You evil, evil child!" She grabbed my arm and pulled me forcefully out of the chair I was sitting in. She flung my arm at the board yelling, "Clear this away now! You stupid, stupid girl!"

I heard her go upstairs. She was banging about in a temper for a while, I hurriedly put my cards etc back in their secret place. I worried that she would tell Dad, and even make it all sound much worse than it was, as I was sure she would enjoy regaling him with tales of how bad and evil I was. However, Dad never mentioned it so I imagine she never told him.

One day there were four of us together in my kitchen, Teresa, Breda, Lyn and myself. Dad was down the bookies, and Mum was out with a friend, so we knew we were alone and safe to set up the Ouija board. We sat giggling, discussing what questions we should ask. Being the age we were, most of our concerns were boy-related. I asked who I was going to marry. The glass spelt out 'Richard Small' and I screamed with laughter. "They must be wrong, the only Richard Small I know is a friend of my brother, and I wouldn't be seen dead with him!" We all laughed and my friends began teasing, calling me 'Mrs Small' and bursting into giggles. Our gaiety however was short lived.

The Spirit controlling the glass appeared to be angered by our reaction. The glass began to move faster as our laughter fell away, replaced by nervous silence – faster and faster. The glass sped in a circle round the Formica table, making a sickening screeching noise that built up to a deafening crescendo. We each had a single finger on the glass, but, as it continued to accelerate, one by one we were unable to keep them on. My friends sat back, recoiling from the spectacle. Suddenly it stopped. As we sat watching in disbelief, it rose up until it was about 18 inches above the table. It remained still in mid air for a few seconds. There was a deadly silence and time seemed to stand still as we all held our breath, scared to look but unable to take our eyes off it. Without warning it exploded, the glass shattered into hundreds of pieces, showering all of us like angry diamonds.

One second later my friends ran screaming from my house and I was left alone, still shaking. I hurriedly cleared away the mess and packed the letters away.

My friends were scared of Spirit after that. Some thought Spirit were bad, others just did not want to talk about it. I was once again without anyone to share my experiences with.

CHAPTER 8

It was 1972, and one of my class mates at secondary school was a boy called Gary; he was friendly and would never hurt a fly. One day he was showing me the cards he had been collecting from tea packets. They were just wild life ones, but he was fascinated with them, and kept them in his pocket to show anyone who took any interest in them.

"Dad says he will take us to a zoo in the summer holidays. I would love to see real wild animals close up," he said enthusiastically.

He lived in a road just off Chiltern Drive and we had the same walk home from school. We reached his house first, and I suppose because I made out I was a little interested in his card collection he said, "Just pop in for a moment, I want to show you some others I've got."

I remember entering his house thinking, what an awful place. It was dirty, dinghy, filthy and neglected with stinking yellow brown net curtains at the window and sticky carpet in the hall.

Looking back, this was what my own house must have looked like to outsiders, but when it is your own it never seems so bad because you are used to it.

A woman's voice came from the living room as we entered the house.

"That you Gary, who yer got wivyer?" she shouted to him.

"It's only a friend I'm showing her me cards," he replied.

"OK but don't be long, I need yer to go get some bread for tea."

Gary led me upstairs; his house was very similar in design to ours, the council had been very busy in the early 1950s, but as I say I felt it was very dirty, and it smelt of old damp clothes and mouldy walls.

He had the smallest bedroom in the house. It was crowded with old furniture: a sideboard and a chest of drawers squashed in at the end of the bed, a wardrobe, and a small table and chair where he said he did his homework. It was so cluttered you could only walk into the door and up alongside the bed. There was no way you could get in easily, either to clean the room or change the bedding, which had obviously not been done for some while.

Gary reached over to his chest of drawers and began shaking and wiggling the top drawer in order to ease it out.

"It's always like this," he said. "There's a knack to it, it won't take a mo."

Sure enough, he managed to get it open wide enough to enable him to get a tin box out. The box looked extremely old; it had once been an emerald green colour, as some remnants of paint were still on it, but in the main it was a mixture of metal and rust, with a catch on it that double-backed on itself to fasten.

Gary quickly and nimbly undid the catch to reveal stacks of cards tied with elastic bands inside.

"Look Susan, these are cards of old war planes, here's a Lancaster bomber!" he almost squealed with delight.

"And these," he said, undoing another elastic band, "these are pop stars!"

I was actually less interested in the pop stars than the war planes, but I replied, "Gary they are great, how did you get so many?"

"Well, I have been collecting them for ages from the tea packets. Dad reckons I have got more than anyone in the country, and that one day they will be worth a lot; I could be a millionaire one day."

I had my doubts, but he was so happy with his treasures I tried to be complimentary. "Well I think you have worked so hard at collecting all this lot, you would deserve to become a millionaire."

"Yeah," he said.

Then the woman's voice again, "Gary, Gary have yer finished? I need you to go to the shop."

We looked at each other. "Dad's girlfriend," he explained.

"Oh, well, I better go now anyway," I said. "Thanks for showing me your cards."

We descended the stairs, and his dad's girlfriend was at the bottom waiting for him. She had a cigarette in her hand, and her badly bleached blonde hair was messy – as if she had backcombed it but had not evened it off afterwards. She had a lot of heavy make-up on with a short skirt and a low cut blouse with frills, but I thought she looked rough, not pretty at all.

She looked at me briefly and nodded a goodbye. As I left I heard her instructing Gary as to what bread she wanted. He shouted, "Bye Susan, see you tomorrow."

After that initial visit to Gary's house, I often walked home with him and sometimes would go in to his house to see his latest collection of things. Some class mates said I fancied him, but believe me nothing was further from the truth. I liked him very much as a friend, that was all. I found him easy to talk to. He listened to me, as I did to him, and although quite often our outlook on things was different, or our taste of TV programmes were at odds, we respected each other's opinion and the right to say what we felt without being victimised or bullied in anyway.

One day Gary and I got talking about ghosts and ghouls whilst walking home. He asked if I had ever watched *Randall and Hopkirk (Deceased)* a TV series about two detectives, one of whom had passed away, but whose ghost came back to help his ex-partner solve crimes. I said I had seen it, and that very often different Spirits came to me and told me stuff. He just laughed, until he saw my face and realised I meant it.

"You are joking Susan – are you mad, you must be dreaming – tell me you are kidding or else!"

"No Gary I ain't kidding. I know most people don't believe me but, the Spirits of dead people do come to me to tell me things or to pass on messages for certain people. You do believe me don't you?" I asked.

Gary looked behind us to see if any other school kids were nearby. "Only if you swear on your life it is true."

"I do swear on my life, honest, Gary. I even passed on messages to my friend's mum and she paid me for it."

"God, ain't you scared!" he exclaimed.

"Well, they don't scare me, I just know they are good, but there are times when some bad ones come and frighten me. I do know the difference then alright."

"Wow!" Gary was impressed, and I could see his mind working; he was ever the one to think up ways of making money.

"Please don't tell anyone at school or I'll be ganged-up on, you know what they are like."

"It will be our secret Susan. Wow," he said again.

The following Friday afternoon Gary asked me to go round his on the way home. He wanted to show me his marble collection. Apparently he had been collecting them over a number of years, and apart from a bad spell of losing marble games when he was between eight and nine years old, he usually won loads more than he lost.

Riveting, I thought.

When we entered his hallway, his dad's girlfriend called out, "Gary, have you got that Susan with you?"

We shot a quick glance at each other, and Gary replied, "Yeah."

"Can you both come in here please," she almost ordered.

We thought we had done something wrong. I could smell alcohol. She was sitting on the sofa in a tracksuit, a glass in one hand and a cigarette in the other. The man standing behind the sofa smiled at us but didn't say anything. There was also a ginger tomcat sitting next to her, but as we entered the room he came up to me to say hello.

As I bent forward to stroke him the woman said, "So tell me Susan about these ghosts you are supposed to see!"

It was said sarcastically, and I was shocked that Gary must have mentioned it to her.

I hesitated and then said, "Well, I don't know really. I mean they just come to me, but they ain't really ghosts they are Spirit."

"What do yer mean, yer don't see 'em flying around with sheets over their heads then!" She laughed loudly.

I just felt embarrassed. The man behind her looked a bit cross, and I continued to stroke the cat.

"What the bloody hell you doing now, love?" she said.

"What's his name?" I asked.

"Whose name?" Gary said.

"The cat of course!" I replied.

Gary looked at me incredulously. "Susan, there hasn't been a cat in the house since my Gingerbread died two years ago!"

I just said, "Oh," and immediately stopped stroking him; however, he still rubbed himself against my legs purring all the while.

The woman almost cackled at this. "She's a nutter Gary you shouldn't go around wiv a nutter!" I felt so stupid, but Gary stuck up for me.

"She is not, she does speak to Spirits and she is not making it up, you don't know her at all!" He was getting upset too, now; he always hated it if anyone got picked on.

As she emptied the glass down her throat she said, "OK Susan, you tell me something from your Spirits that you couldn't know 'bout me, and I will believe it."

The man standing behind the sofa suddenly said to me, "Tell her she knows the answer, she should leave and live somewhere else." I told her this.

She shouted, "What the hell do you mean?"

He spoke to me again, and I told her. "He says 'Silvie Socks', you know what to do."

There was a stunned silence in which she seemed to drop the empty glass in slow motion, whilst her mouth opened ever wider, but she was unable to speak at first.

When she did, she said, "Oh my God!" and ran from the room.

Next time I went round Gary's house his dad's girlfriend no longer lived there.

CHAPTER 9

I woke up one morning in June with a horrible feeling of doom again. I tried to keep things to myself when I got these feelings as Dad would get very annoyed and send me to my room as punishment for talking to dead people.

However, this particular day I could not shake the feeling, and in fact it seemed to get worse and worse as the day wore on. In the afternoon I went to my bedroom to try to catch up on some homework. As soon as I sat on my bed, I was being shown a vivid picture in my mind: much more than a dream, it was just like watching television. The uneasy feeling I had had all the morning was now stronger than ever.

I saw and heard a plane crashing into our house; it was so real I just knew it was going to happen. The noise was horrendous and the feeling of fear and panic I felt made me want to vomit. It was definitely, definitely real.

I knew Dad did not like me telling him things, but I was so convinced we were all going to be killed at any moment that I had to tell him.

Dad was out at the shops, but as soon as he came in I told him. He told me to stop with all that and go to my room. He said that unless I stopped it, I would not be coming down for tea. I went up to my room, feeling sick and terrified – I did not know how to make anyone listen to me, and I certainly did not feel like eating anyway.

When bedtime came Dad came upstairs to say goodnight to me. I think he was hoping I would say sorry or something so that he could give me a jam sandwich. I felt just as sure as ever, and I told him again that it was going to happen. He just shouted at me saying, "It's wrong to talk to dead people, they are evil!" and stormed out of the bedroom.

I somehow got some sleep that night, and when I awoke in the morning the first thing I noticed was that the bad feeling had disappeared. I thought, 'Thank God for that.' I was hungry and got up and got some breakfast. Dad was out.

When he returned he was in a foul mood. I heard him ask where I was, and then he came into the kitchen.

He really shouted at me, almost spitting with fury and anger, "You, you made it happen!"

I stood up and said, "What, what's happened?"

"The plane, the plane, it crashed four miles away, it's your fault! How many times have I told you not to talk to dead people – they are from the Devil and are making you do the Devil's work!"

He continued, "If you ever do it again God knows what you will make me do – go to your room and stay there!"

I ran upstairs crying uncontrollably. What if he was right? I know I didn't make it happen, but how did I know beforehand? I threw myself onto the bed and lay there crying desperately. Michael came and sat on the edge of the bed. I did not know how to feel about him now. Was it wrong to speak to Spirit? I loved my dad with all my heart – to see him so angry and upset because of me, hurt like mad. At that moment I was lost and did not know what to think. I turned to Michael and said, "Just go away!"

I found out later that evening, 18th June 1972 that 118 people were killed in a plane. Shortly after taking off at Heathrow, it crashed in a field in Staines.

My house felt very quiet over the next few days. I had not realised how busy it normally was with Spirit. I began to miss them very much; it felt like a part of me was missing. After three days I could not stand the emptiness anymore. I went up to my room and said in my head, "Michael, if you are still there, please come back to me. I know I need you and I am so very sorry for asking you to go away."

With that, Michael appeared next to me. I was so happy and relieved. From then on I would never ask him to leave me again.

One afternoon, two weeks later, Joe and I were arguing about music. We liked different things and both wanted to play the records we liked the best. We called a truce and decided I would play one I like then he could play one he liked etc.

When it was my turn I turned the volume up really loud, as teenagers who love their music do. Joe left the front room in a bit of a huff; he would not even entertain the idea of listening to one of the records I liked.

When my record had finished, I turned around to shout to Joe that he could now play his. To my surprise Father O'Toole was standing next to me. Not only did I jump out of my skin, but I felt somewhat embarrassed as I had been singing at the top of my voice.

He said, "Hello Susan."

I said, "Oh hello, Father."

"I hear you have been talking again to people you should not be talking to."

Joe was standing behind Father O'Toole making faces at me. Father O'Toole asked me a few questions, which I answered honestly.

He then lunged forward, and produced a bottle of Holy Water, and started talking in a different language. He raised the bottle and performed the sign of the cross towards me. Then, to my amazement, he splashed me in the face with the water! He kept on splashing me, and I looked at Joe, who was standing behind him, for help. However, Joe was not about to help me in any way. He was silently laughing at me, with his hand clamped over his mouth. When I saw this it made me laugh, and Father O'Toole got rather angry. I was by this time getting soaked.

We heard Dad coming in the front door. Father O'Toole just told me I was a very naughty girl and he rushed out to see Dad.

I heard him saying frantically to Dad, "There's no helping her!" and he left our house immediately.

I thought to myself, what on earth does he think is wrong with me? I feel normal, just a little wet.

Joe was still laughing. I never saw Father O'Toole again.

October 1972 was very bad for all of us. I got in from school one afternoon soaked through, as there had been extremely heavy rain on the way home, and I only had Eve's old blue padded anorak to wear. This was now short on me, and my school skirt was thin. I must have looked a state. Mum spoke kindly to me when she saw me. "Oh dear Susan, you look very cold and wet, love. Get those things off and I'll make you a cup of tea," she said.

"Thanks Mum, that'll be nice," I replied. I was thinking it was unusual for her to even notice I had got in, let alone make me a cup of tea, but I went upstairs and took all my clothes off as even my knickers were soaked through. I hurriedly put on a dress and cardigan and went downstairs to get the cup of tea Mum was making for me. I felt there was something I needed to do most urgently, but I did not know what: something I really needed to see and understand.

As usual I almost flew down the stairs, because the negative Spirit were very active at this time and I could rarely go upstairs at this age without them trying to frighten me on the way down. Mum called to me from the kitchen, "Tea's in here Susan love."

'Love,' I thought. 'What is going on?'

I sat down at the sticky Formica kitchen table next to Mum, old, wet tea dribbles on the surface mixed with fag ash.

She asked, "How did school go today dear?"

"Fine," I said. "Science was boring because the teacher was sick, so we just had to read our books for two hours."

She was not interested in my school day really; I knew she hadn't even listened to my answer.

"Well, we are having pie and potatoes tonight, and I wondered if you would like to learn how to make my gravy?" she asked. I hesitated for just a second because I had never known Mum to show me how to do anything before. In fact if ever I asked she would either say, 'Not right now' or 'I Don't have time' something like that.

She said, "Well I could show Eve, but she is working full time and, as you know, gets home late, I expect she just wants her dinner then."

"Oh no, Mum, I mean yes, I want to learn how to do it," and, as an afterthought, "everyone loves 'Mum's gravy' best." Mum was no good at cooking at all – probably because she never got much practice. However, she did make a lovely thick rich gravy, and, if you have a small meal, dipping a slice of bread into that gravy filled you up.

So after I had finished my tea, Mum taught me how she did the gravy, and at dinner time I did it on my own. We dished out the shop-bought individual steak and kidney pies. Mum and Dad had one each, and the four of us had half of one each. Then we did the mash potato, and lastly the gravy. Mum and I didn't let on to anyone else that I had made the gravy, and everyone ate it all without realising that I had done it.

"Well," said Mum when we had all finished, "I have to congratulate Susan. She made 'my gravy' today and no one noticed, so she must of made it as well as I do!"

"Oh, well done," said Eve. "Even I can't do that yet, Susie Coo."

"It was very nice love," Dad said.

Joe and Andy just grunted, but it seemed like an appreciative grunt to me.

I remember feeling proud about it, but more bewildered that Mum had actually wanted to show me something, when it was just me and her doing it. I still had a feeling of urgently needing to understand something.

The following Saturday night I found out what it was.

It was late at night or the early hours of the morning, when Mum came and woke us all up and told us to go downstairs. When we were all in the front room, Mum and

Dad told us to sit down as they had something important to tell us.

Then they dropped the bombshell. They were going to get divorced. I was devastated, I couldn't speak and the room seemed to be spinning around me.

When it registered with us, we were all crying. I thought it meant that Dad was going to leave us. My stomach seemed like it was being cut out of my body, and my heart was threatening to pound out from my chest. All hell seemed to be let loose with lots of noise, crying, pleading and questions.

Eve went over to cuddle Andy, and she said, "Stop it, stop it, this is too much for him." Andy was crying and he was shaking all over, almost as if he was having a fit. He tried to breathe between gulps of air, and he had wet himself. I don't think he totally realised the implications of what was going on, but he knew it was the worst thing that ever, ever happened to us.

Joe was crying quietly by now and clinging onto Mum's dress at the waist. Eve looked so white and she began to sweat. Although I was hurting so bad myself, when I looked at her I thought she was going to vomit any second.

Then Mum said, very coldly and clearly, "I have a boyfriend and I want to be with him so I am leaving."

Dad started crying then, as we all began wailing again – I saw the tears rolling down his cheeks.

Eve shouted, "Bitch!" at Mum, and left the room dragging Andy with her.

I could not say anything. I felt a strong hatred towards Mum, but I did not want her to go. I wanted to give Dad a hug, but I was frozen to the spot. Dad had his head in his hands and

Joe would not let go of Mum's dress. Mum just looked past me. She had a stern and determined look in her eye.

Eventually Dad stopped sobbing, and turned to me and Joe and said, "Go to bed now kids, we will sort things out in the morning."

We did as we were told. Mum never looked at me, and she only touched Joe to enable her to undo his hand, which was clutching desperately at her arm. To this day I cannot believe that. If ever she thought Dad favoured me as a little 'miracle' or whatever, then she equally favoured Joe. To think she showed no emotion, even to him at that time, makes my blood run cold even now.

The next morning when we got up, she had already left to be with her boyfriend Calvert. We didn't see her go, she did not even say goodbye to us.

It was a very long time before we saw her again.

I was only thirteen then, but none of us could understand what we had done to make Mum want to leave us. However, it was a great relief to me that Dad stayed. My only real concern was whether or not we would eat. Although Dad had a full-time job at this point, he was used to spending most of his money down the bookies. However, Mum leaving seemed to change him overnight. He started to behave like a responsible parent, and with his wages and a bit from Eve as her 'rent', now that she was working, we managed.

I knew that Dad loved Mum very, very much, and night after night I heard him crying alone in his room. It broke my heart to hear it, and I swore then that, whatever happened in my life, I would never, never be unfaithful to anyone.

Dad paid me fifty pence a week for doing the household chores, and cooking dinner every night. I often thought back to Mum having taught me how to make her gravy just a few days before she left, and I never felt like making it like that again. I made 'my' gravy which was not as thick, but just as tasty.

After Mum left, Dad always made sure that there was food on the table for us, which was good, and it was a novelty to be able to have a jam sandwich anytime you wanted. But he had lost a lot of his faith; there was no longer any pressure for us to go to church every week. Eve had already had an argument with him, and said she was old enough to make up her own mind about her God. She confided in me that working all week, earning money and going out on a Saturday night meant she needed a lie-in on Sundays!

Although Dad's faith seemed to have dwindled somewhat, he still did not like me talking to dead people, so I kept it to myself when I did. Eve, Joe and Andy were all frightened of the dead and what 'ghosts' could do. I could never understand their fear, because I always found I could rely on the Spirit world; they never let me down, not like living people. Not like Mum.

All of us suffered in one way or another when Mum just upped and left. All of us were affected in different ways. Joe, who was already bullied at school for being quiet and small for his age, withdrew into himself more and more. He seemed to walk about in a daze with a vague look about him.

Eve changed in as much as she hated Mum so much that she denied any feelings of wanting to ever see her again or even caring if she were alive. She became angry at odd times and for odd reasons; she had never been like it before Mum left.

I was devastated and had mixed feelings. I wanted Mum back desperately, but I hated her for hurting Dad so much. I guess I just wanted things to go back to how they were before.

Andy was most obviously and immediately having difficulty coming to terms with it at all.

Dad and Eve went to work about eight in the mornings. Dad left it to me to ensure Andy got off to school alright, and to see him across the road before I went. Andy went in one direction to primary, and I and Joe in the other to the secondary school.

Every morning I would try to get him to go to school, but we usually only got a little way across the field before he broke away from me and ran away. I would shout and scream at him to come back; I needed to get to school myself and he should not be roaming the streets. He would not do as I asked, and every day I just had to go off to school knowing he could get hurt, or worse, while I was away.

Dad had long discussions with him about how important it was for him to go to school: how he would get into deep trouble if he did not attend, and even that the Welfare people might take him away if he would not go to school.

Every night he promised he would behave and go the next day. Every day the same scenario would be played out. He lost about six months schooling before the Welfare stepped in. I now think they must have realised how traumatised he was by Mum leaving. Thank God they did not take him away; I was so frightened they would.

They arranged for a Child Psychologist to see him. After a couple of weeks of that, the whole family (what was left of us anyway) were invited into the sessions. They seemed to just be asking us questions and talking to us all. However, they got to the bottom of it, though I didn't feel you had to be a professional to work it out. He kept running away because he wanted to hide in the Pit all day, without food or water, to see if Mum came back. He was so traumatised that she did not say goodbye that he wanted to make sure that if she even just popped back for some clothes he would not miss seeing her. He had planned to hold onto her so tight that she could never get away.

I do not remember how they got him to go back to school, but he did eventually settle and attend school most days. He was behind the other kids but he was quite an intelligent lad and caught up on his studies. It was a very bad time for him, and like all of us the repercussions live on in our lives to this day.

CHAPTER 10

Christmas 1972 was a non-event that was cold and sad, though Eve and Dad did try to make it a bit better. Eve bought us all a little present for the first time, as she was working now. Dad bought the same old compendium of games as a joint present, and colouring and crossword books for us individually. However, he made sure we had plenty to eat this year, including a turkey. But no Mum.

Come 1973, the loss of Mum from our lives was obviously still having a great effect on all of us. Some days the gnawing, agonising anger and grief became unbearable. This was when the light shows really helped me through and enabled me to at least sleep peacefully.

At night I would look into the bottom of my glass lemonade (hot water) bottle. When I was younger the 'lights' had shown me fairies and ballet dancers, but now I would see lots of small lights in my bedroom. Some of them were whizzing around fast, some floating gently past. Yet others came so close to my face I felt they were looking at me.

I always had a lovely, calm and pleasant feeling when the lights were about, and they helped me forget about Mum, at least for a while.

Michael explained to me that these lights were called orbs, and that each orb was a Spirit. He told me the ones whizzing about were just young, playful and happy Spirit. It was just an easy way for Spirit to get through to me. They can vary in size, but are usually fairly small, about the size of a ten pence piece.

I have seen these lights every day of my life since, even yesterday at Eve's house whilst writing this book.

Although at this time I had lots of kindly Spirit trying to help me through my emotional pain I was aware that negative Spirit were in some sort of battle to win my attention. However, even at this relatively young age, I was becoming accustomed to the 'threats' some negative Spirit tried to display to me, just in order to frighten me. It was as if it were a game on their part. Sometimes it still worked on me: others I just felt annoyed about.

One morning I had been downstairs, had my Daddy's sauce sandwich for breakfast and returned to my bedroom to get dressed for school. I was heading straight for the wardrobe to get my school uniform out, when my bedroom door slammed shut behind me. As I turned around to see what was going on, the bedside table began moving across the floor, making quite a drama out of it, screeching and juddering along all by itself. It appeared to be trying to head for the door in order to prevent me getting out of the room. I just told them (the negative Spirit) off, saying: "I really don't have time for these silly games today," as I moved the table back into place myself.

Looking back, I now realise I should never have been so patronising towards Spirit, even negative Spirit. I have since learnt how to correctly deal with the bad Spirits.

We had an old upright piano in our front room. Since Mum had left us, if I were on my own in the house, I would often hear someone playing it. This did not frighten me, but I thought better than to disturb them. On one particular occasion, the music was so beautiful, peaceful even, it lifted my heart. I had to find out who was playing it. I walked into the room but when I looked there was no one there! The music stopped. I said, "Don't stop, its good." Nothing happened, but as I turned around to walk back out of the room, one key was struck in acknowledgement. There were many times when it felt totally natural, and I was at ease with Spirit like this.

I had been so traumatised by the recent events in our family that I spent most of the year on autopilot. I was just going through the motions of life.

My fourteenth birthday, July 1973, came and went, still not a word from Mum. Dad did not know where she lived or even how to contact her in an emergency. All Mum's family had severed links with us at this time. At least Uncle Charlie could not eat food off our plates if he wasn't there.

I continued to make some pocket money by doing sittings for my friends' mums and their mums' friends too. By the time the summer holidays were over I had made quite a tidy sum. I could never let Dad know of course, so I hid the money in my bedroom, and only spent it sparingly so he would not ask questions.

During these holidays I remember a reading I did for a friend's aunty who had just moved into the other end of Chiltern Drive. It was a Saturday afternoon, and my friend Madeline knocked on the door and asked me if I could go straight away to do a sitting for her aunty who was very upset. I had just finished preparing the dinner so I told her I could spare about ten minutes. Madeline seemed quite agitated and upset herself as we hurried up the road.

When I entered her aunty's house, I immediately had a bad feeling. Within seconds I felt pressure on my neck which tightened and I could not speak. The aunty was firing questions at me in a blind panic, and I asked Michael to help me as I could not talk.

As Madeline showed me into the lounge she said, "Aunty calm down, give Susan a minute." She gestured me to sit down and her aunty followed. The aunty began to talk again, this time less frantically. She told me that since she had moved in a couple of weeks ago strange things were happening and she was frightened by them, especially living on her own. She explained that she kept seeing things moving at the edge of her vision, but when she turned for a clear view there was nothing to see, just an icy breeze in the room. She told me that when she put the light on some evenings it would actually go off again at the switch. She had an electrician in who said it was impossible and all the electrics were fine. She often heard strange noises, creaking and shuffling, as if someone else were in the house, and often doors would open and shut on their own. Then last night in bed she felt someone was strangling her, but no one was there. She said she was sure the house was haunted and felt that she could not stay there any longer, but had nowhere else to go.

I remember thinking, 'Crikes, what can I do about it?'

I said, "OK, yes there is a Spirit here..." she let out a scream before I could continue – it made me jump – and she and Madeline jumped too!

I said, "No, it's OK, it's not bad."

"Well it bloody well feels bad to me – can you get rid of it?"

"I don't know. It's a young man; I will try to talk to him and see if I can help."

In my mind I asked Michael, who was standing next to me, to help.

"Why is he here and what should I do?"

Michael said, "Just talk to him like you said."

The young man entered the lounge. He looked a shocking sight: his face had black and purple bruises all over it, and his eyes were bulging. He had what appeared to be a long scarf around his neck. It was obvious that neither Madeline nor her aunty could see him. He was looking straight at me, so I said, "Hello, what are you doing here?"

"I live here, well er, I did, this is my home not hers!" He shot a look at Madeline's aunty, who immediately shuddered.

"I died up there," he said pointing to the bedroom upstairs.

"I see, but this is her house now, why are you still here?"

"I am looking for my mum and dad, but I can't find them." Tears began to fall from his bulging eyes.

I looked at Michael, and he told me, "Tell him they have moved. I know where they are and I will take him to them. He must not stay here any longer."

I told the young man this. He seemed to double-up in anguish and put his arm out towards me – Michael grabbed his hand and then they were both gone.

"Good, that's it," I said to Madeline's aunty.

"What do you mean, it's gone?"

"Yes he has, he will be OK now, and so will you."

She looked doubtful – I said, "Just see tonight, I promise you he's gone for good."

Two days later Madeline knocked our front door again. This time it was with a large, very prettily wrapped, box of chocolates from her aunty as a 'Thank You' gift.

By the time I returned to school in September 1973, I believed I was over the hurt of Mum going, and if I thought of her it was only with a sense of disgust. No way was I ever over it – not even to this day!

One day, in the second week of term, I was walking to school and I suddenly got a picture of my Uncle John in my mind. I could not stop thinking of him all day.

My Uncle John passed away two years before this, in 1971,when I was twelve years old. I always liked him: he always seemed a cheerful and a happy man. He was only 48 years old when he died – far too young. We sometimes went to visit him and Aunty Beryl, who was one of Mum's older sisters, together with their daughter, my cousin June. Whenever we arrived at their house, I remember it always smelt of polish, lavender furniture polish – very strong, but bearable because Aunty Beryl always made lovely sandwiches. Any sandwiches were a bonus, but she did things like ham with tomato, cheese with pickle and sometimes salmon paste! Better than Christmas in Chiltern Drive. Our visits to Aunty Beryl's house became fewer and fewer after he died, but to this day I have never forgotten him and his kindly way.

Because Uncle John had been on my mind all day, I went straight to the nearest phone box on my way home from school and phoned my Aunty Beryl. A man answered the phone, and I asked to speak to my aunty. I told her that I had been thinking of Uncle John all day, and it made me feel I should ring her.

She said, "Today is the anniversary of the day he died – thanks very much for reminding me!" She seemed annoyed or upset and just put the phone down on me. I felt devastated; I was trying to be nice to her and ended up causing trouble.

I walked home, feeling upset. As soon as I opened the door I was immediately hit by a strong smell of lavender furniture polish. I went into the front room, and Uncle John was sitting on the sofa. I said, "Hello," and told him how much I missed him, and that he could come and see me whenever he wanted to.

He nodded and smiled at me, his unmistakable happy, happy smile. Then he said, "She's getting married you know." He blew me a kiss and got up and left.

A few weeks later we heard through Uncle Charlie that Aunty Beryl had met a man called Derek, who was a widower with a son called Paul. Aunty Beryl and June were going to move into his house with him.

Sure enough, a few weeks after that we heard they had got married.

CHAPTER 11

Joe and I would walk home from school at lunchtime to get ourselves some lunch. As I've mentioned, the time when Dad could claim free school meals had long since passed for us, and the cost of a meal at school was still too much.

Most days we would have a can of soup between us, and then walk back to school for afternoon lessons.

This particular day I went to the pantry for a can of chicken soup. Just as my hand reached in to get it, Joe said to me, "Look at this!" – there was a dead mouse on the floor under the kitchen table. As my attention was drawn to the mouse, I suddenly got a hard slap on the hand from within the pantry, which made me jump and shout in alarm much more than the dead mouse did.

"What?" shouted Joe, just as loudly.

"Something slapped my hand!" I exclaimed.

"Don't be daft, don't start," he said. "Something must of fell off the shelf."

"Well you find out what it was then,' cos I ain't," I said.

"I won't waste my time on such nonsense," was all he said.

Then Joe got rid of the mouse, using an old newspaper, and threw it over the back garden fence into the Pit. We thought Pixie must have brought it in. We had lunch, and I noticed even Joe, who has always tried to deny any Spirits exist, kept an eye on the pantry as we ate.

At this time, on the way home after school, we would collect Andy from his friend David's house. David's mum kindly watched over him for half an hour each day, until we picked him up. Andy was still at juniors, being about ten years old, and Dad would not let him have his own key to the house yet.

The day something slapped my hand in the pantry, all three of us got in and walked into the kitchen to make a cup of tea. We found all the cupboard doors, drawers and even the pantry door were open. As we had all walked into the kitchen together, Joe could not deny we had not left the house like it at lunchtime. We were both speechless.

Andy said, "Crikes, we've been burgled!"

Nothing had been taken, no external doors or windows had been opened, but the unsettling feeling I call the Dreads was all around us.

Dad got in from work and insisted it must have been some ruffians who got in and did it. We all tidied up, but I know Joe, although he would not admit it, thought it might be ghosts.

Eve was rushing to go out after work so did not take in the possibility it may have been a Spirit. She checked all her clothes and handbags were still in the bedroom and went out. I did not tell her what I thought, or about the slap I got from something in the pantry at lunchtime.

In early 1974, I realised, to my great surprise, I could help Spirit as well as living people. I had already begun to acknowledge the good effect my readings had on people, especially when I was given messages from Spirit about someone's life that I could not have known of previously. Some people are so desperate to believe, that whatever you say would be beneficial, but usually my readings proved the truth beyond doubt. This did become a bit of a problem sometimes like I was busy doing homework, and a friend would come round and ask me to do a sitting for their granny or mum's next door neighbour. However, on the plus side, I was never short of a bit of pocket money.

One afternoon, when I got in from school, Joe went almost straight back out to go round to a mate's house, and Andy had been invited to stay at David's for tea. I got on and prepared the vegetables and potatoes for dinner. Afterwards I put my feet up on the sofa and was soon asleep. In the dream that followed, I saw a man of about thirty-five floating above me. His left ear had been severed, and dried blood was all over the left side of his face and his jacket. In his right hand he was wielding a large knife that seemed to curve at the end. I felt as one does in the middle of a nightmare, frightened and trying to wake myself up – almost aware it is a dream but still needing to get away.

He started waving the knife at me. He was extremely agitated, and he said in a gravelly, deep and terrifying voice, "I'm not going, no one is going to make me, not even someone like you!" I woke up with a start as he thrust the knife towards me.

I was shaking and thought, 'Thank God that was just a dream,' when I realised he was still there, floating above me and looking as angry as ever. I scrambled off the sofa, and as I was running into the kitchen I called out, "Michael, help me!"

Michael appeared in front of me immediately. I asked him to make the man go away. He said, "I will, just as soon as you have helped him."

"Michael he wants to kill me!" I shouted.

"He cannot hurt you Susan, and I cannot help him by myself, I need you on this one. He needs a living Spirit to guide him on his way."

"Well how can I help?" I shook. "I am scared of the way he is threatening me."

"You trust me don't you, Susan?" he replied, and put his hand on my shoulder. I instantly felt calm and knew Michael was teaching me something important.

I felt it was right to try and help this man, and I said, "Yes, Michael I do trust you, but I don't know how to help him."

"Come on," he said, and guided me back into the front room still resting his hand on my shoulder.

The man was sitting in an armchair; he looked completely shocked, dazed and unable to see what had happened to him. He still held the knife, and as I entered the room he lifted it up towards me, this time though it was more in defence than attack. As his arm moved forward I noticed for the first time he had a large knife wound to the chest, as well as the missing left ear.

I sat down on the sofa opposite him, with Michael at my side. Michael said, "Just talk to him." I did not know what to say or what was expected from me, but once I began the words just seemed to flow.

"My name is Susan and I want to help you," I said.

His angry and confused voice roared at me, "What the f... what is happening here? I could kill you in a moment!"

"You have been in a fight with another man – it was only ten minutes ago," I continued.

He went to speak again, but I was already talking. "You do remember that don't you, fighting with this other guy?"

He nodded in disbelief, his Spirit at that moment was the most lost, anguished and terrible soul I had seen in my fourteen years. I yearned to reach out to him; this aggressive threatening adult with blood all over him needed me. I had to continue to explain what Spirit compelled me to say.

"The other guy won, you were fatally wounded, look at your chest," I said.

He looked down slowly. He seemed to understand, but it was too much to take in all at once.

He eventually looked back up at me. "Please, please tell me I am not dead; I don't want to go anywhere else, please help me!"

"You are dead, but because it was so sudden your Spirit was parted from your physical being without warning; that is why it is so hard to believe."

"Oh God, Oh God, no, no please!" he screamed and cried. It was very distressing for me as well, and I felt sick to the core. Michael squeezed at my shoulder again, which gave me the strength to carry on even though he was wailing in grief.

"You can stay with me until you accept what has happened. I can only tell you it is not something to be frightened of. It is just different, spiritual not physical – you will be alright and you will be with those you love and those that love you."

"Michael," I said, "he is too distressed to hear what I am saying."

Michael said it was OK; he had heard me even though he was in turmoil at the moment. He told me to carry on explaining.

"It is only sudden, violent death that brings this traumatised transition to the Spirit world," I said – not really understanding myself. "For most people it is but a natural step from one room to the next."

His wailing was eventually taken over by a childlike sobbing; he could not stop himself. But he looked up at me when I said, "You will come to terms with it, and you will be with your family soon."

"What about my wife and kids? They are alive, and if I am dead how can I be with them?"

I replied, "In a few moments when you feel better your guides will show you how to be with them."

"Who are you?" he sobbed.

"I am just me and I am trying to help you understand, look behind you."

He turned around and dropped his knife to the floor when he saw an old woman with open arms. "Gran," he said, "it's you!" They cuddled each other very tightly. When they finished embracing, I noticed all the blood on him had disappeared and his left ear was back.

In that moment he seemed to realise; he knew his grandmother had died ten years ago, yet he could feel her, hold her and talk to her. She led him away; he turned and waved at me. I never saw him again.

I felt more exhausted than before I had dropped off to sleep. I also felt overwhelmed by the experience. Michael assured me I did good. I just wanted to know this sort of thing wouldn't keep happening to me.

"No," Michael said, "I would not let you deal with more than you are able to, but from time to time you may need to help the dead as well as the living."

Joe entered the front room then and said, "What's for dinner?"

I also had at this time a very frightening, recurring incident that negative Spirit seemed to enjoy inflicting on me. This happened fairly regularly between the ages of fourteen and nineteen. I remember the first time because it was Eve's birthday, February 1974. When I had been asleep for some while, I woke up, but could not open my eyes. I could not speak or make a sound or even move any part of my body. I tried desperately to move my arms or legs, but just could not.

Next I would hear someone breathing heavily, and then a breeze would brush across my face. I tried so hard to shout out, to open my eyes – nothing would work, but I was totally conscious of my surroundings. Then I heard a wind in my ears and someone was holding me down, pinning me down to the bed. It was as if they were lying on top of me, heavy and almost crushing me.

Michael came and helped me talk to the negative Spirit to get them to leave me be. I was often close to panic at these times, and Michael helped to keep me calm. However, it was usually a good ten minutes before I could even open my eyes, let alone move.

In April, after eighteen months of nothing, no notes, no letters, no Christmas wishes, not even the desperately hoped for birthday cards she might have remembered to send, Mum just turned up on the doorstep. She obviously thought we would be pleased to see her and everything would be OK.

Andy was so happy to see her; he just cried and cried. He could not believe his mum was here again, after all his prayers and longings night after night, day after day. A broken child if ever there was one. I was extremely worried about him and the balance of his mind. I just shouted at her to go away, that we did not need her or want her back!

What made things worse, I felt, was that Dad seemed happy to see her. I just could not understand: I felt like I had been there to pick up the pieces when she deserted us, and now he was welcoming her back. She was having problems with Calvert, and Dad let her stay a few days – he even slept on the sofa so she could have his bed!

She was back with us about a week. She told Andy if she ever left again she would at least tell him and say where she was. Perhaps even she realised how much he had suffered – perhaps she even cared?

This was found to be not so, as she just disappeared one day, leaving a note to Dad. 'Calvert and I are trying again' was all it said. I found this time I did miss her. When she was there she did at least cook some meals, which helped me out.

I did love her, after all she was my mother, but I was still very angry at what she had put us all through.

This time however, even though she did not tell us to our face she was leaving again, she did at least pop in to see us once or twice a week. This helped Andy a lot I know, because he was at a difficult age, moving up to secondary school and needing to feel secure.

On one of these visits to us she brought lots of bottles of lotion. We had all been scratching and itching all over. This lotion was to treat scabies, a mite that burrows under your skin and can travel all around the body if not treated.

It turned out that she had brought it into our house because she had been sleeping in filthy conditions with Calvert. It is passed on by physical contact, and it is also possible to catch it from someone if you use the same towel or bedding.

The lotion stank to high heaven and we all had to be 'painted' from head to toe with it to ensure the mites were all eradicated.

I remember the lotion also stung, we even had to put it on our 'privates'. Thanks Calvert, thanks Mother!

Several weeks later, Dad received a phone call from the local hospital to say Mum had been admitted. We all went to visit her, and we were shocked at the state she was in. She had been beaten black and blue by her boyfriend. Her face was almost unrecognisable, and she had tubes coming from her nose and arm. All she could say was, "Oh, Arthur, what have I done." She had been kicked so badly in the abdomen she had to have a hysterectomy.

When Mum came out of hospital she came back to us in Chiltern Drive once again, initially to recuperate from her operation, but she stayed longer this time. Eve, who had gone from a blinding hate of Mum to absolute total indifference, just said, "It's only 'cos she has nowhere else – she is using Dad again."

When we questioned Dad about his continued concern for Mum, after all she had done to him (and us), he just said, "I love her, and I forgive her everything."

This was November 1974. I was in the last year of school. Although Joe had had a job for a while he was presently on the dole. Eve worked at the same company as her new fiancé, and none of us saw much of her, as she popped home from work just to eat dinner and get ready to go out with him.

Andy was just so happy Mum was home again, even though she was not well. I felt a little betrayed by Dad again, but only a little: I know he never stopped loving her. Maybe it was his religious beliefs that made him able to forgive her anything. I believe it was his true, devoted love for her – although it was never reciprocated.

Christmas came and went – Mum and Dad made sure Andy had plenty of little presents to open, and Mum ordered me, Joe and Eve clothes from a catalogue. Dad bought Mum a gold cross and chain in a beautiful presentation box.

"Oh Arthur, thank you, I really didn't think we would buy for each other, sorry," was all she said.

By the middle of January 1975, Mum was totally recovered although she did not seem to be looking for anywhere else to live or any job to do. She was living off Dad really, but Andy seemed so at ease and able to enjoy each day knowing she would be there when he got home from school.

Mum eventually started to go out with 'friends' again in the evening, and in March 1975 she told Dad she had met a very special man called Thomas and was going to move in with him. She said they were madly in love with each other, and although she was sorry to be going again she really had no choice. She swore to Andy she was only going to be living ten minutes away and would come and see him lots. He asked if he could please go with her, but she said, "Maybe in a few weeks I'll see."

She never did let Andy live with her but he was allowed round to Thomas' house a few times. However, he never got on with him so usually waited to see her when she visited Chiltern Drive.

Having Mum back home for a year meant that we still missed her when she left again, but we were older. As they say, the first cut is the deepest. Although Andy was again the most affected, she at least kept in regular contact with him this time.

In May I went for an interview at a well-known boutique in Slough, and Michael came with me for support. The interview went well, and I got the job to start the following week. Only thing was I hadn't finished school yet. When I went into school the following day I had a word with the teacher, and they sorted it out so that I could leave the following Friday.

I had only been working at the boutique in the town a couple of weeks when something happened on the bus one morning. I was idly looking out of the window when I noticed a young lad of about ten years old holding a bunch of roses. He was standing on the pavement and, as the bus went by, he was staring straight at me.

Then I was aware that the bus driver had sounded his horn at someone on the road in front of him, which made me turn my head to the front of the bus. The bus carried on at about twenty-five miles an hour, and when I looked back out of the window again I saw the same boy, with the same roses, standing by the edge of the pavement. He waved at me and I smiled. This I thought was impossible, but just as I thought it, he was sitting next to me on the bus. I realised that he was a Spirit and I said, "Hello, they are lovely flowers."

He said, "Could you give them to my mum and tell her I am alright?"

I replied, "Yes, I will if you tell me where she is."

He pointed towards the front of the bus, but then he vanished. Unfortunately there were a few women at the front of the bus so I could not tell which one was his mum.

I became aware that the woman opposite me was giving me very strange looks, as if I were mad. I had been talking to myself as far as she was concerned.

Another lesson learned: when out in public on my own I must talk to Spirit in my mind, so that the living cannot hear me.

A couple of week later, I was waiting for the bus to go to work when I heard someone say "Hello" to me, but when I turned around there was nobody there.

The bus turned up and it was packed. I could see an empty seat towards the back of the bus. I made my way through the people to get to the seat and sat down. The lady sitting next to me was in her forties; she smiled at me then turned her head to look out of the window.

I was thinking about the day ahead of me, when I was aware of Spirit trying to get through to me. I looked up and saw the young boy with the roses again. He was standing right next to me in the aisle of the bus.

He said, "I'm, Tim, that's my Mum," and gestured to the lady I was sitting next to.

'Oh,' I thought.

He then asked me to give her the roses and to tell her he loved her very much, and went to visit her every day.

I said I would, but I didn't know how to pass on this message; it wasn't really the time or place. I knew we were coming to the end of our journey, so I had to think fast. The bus pulled into the station and we all got off.

I decided to approach the lady, and after a few moments of deliberation, I said, "I don't know how to put this, but... do you believe in life after death?"

She looked at me as if she didn't know what to say. So I just blurted it out.

"I have a message for you from Tim, your son." The lady started to shake. I said, "He's giving you a lovely bunch of pink roses, and he wants me to tell you that he loves you and see you every day."

Tim then said, "Tell her happy birthday." So I did.

A tear rolled down her cheek. I told her he was with her every day, so if she talked to him, he would hear her. She nodded. I gave her a quick hug and rushed off to work. If I had more time, I would have been able to talk to her for longer, but I was already running late.

From that moment on, I realised it was my duty to deliver messages from Spirit to their loved ones. Through doing this, I could see my gift of communicating with the Spirit world could bring so much comfort and peace to those of us still living.

I only wished I had listened to their messages and guidance that were meant personally for me...

Now read my next book **Both Worlds 2**, which tells of my life between the ages of sixteen and thirty-seven. I meet and marry an abusive, controlling partner, and have two wonderful children. This second book demonstrates how I develop spiritually, how I began to do more and more sittings for people and met other mediums through a spiritual church. As I grew in Spirit most of my time was devoted to readings for people .By the age of thirty-seven I realised how Spirit had helped me to survive the darkest days of my life.

Here's the first chapter…

1975 – 1976

I settled into the job very quickly and made many new friends, but became particularly close to Avril and Odette. We got on really well, and went out most weekends together and it was fun.

Avril and Odette often mentioned they were afraid to go through the stock room on the second floor, but had to do this to get to the third floor staff room upstairs. It was a bit dark and spooky and there was a resident male Spirit who thought it was funny to slam doors and pinch your bum as you walked through.

One day the manager, Julie, had a very frightening experience in the staff room. She came down into the shop as white as a ghost, almost crying. When she managed to speak she gestured to me, saying, "It's only started to happen since you worked here!"

Avril and Odette burst out laughing and I said, "It's not my fault." Odette said that it had been happening at least since she had been there and that was two years prior to my arrival.

We asked her what happened, and she told us that somebody kept pushing her as she ran down the stairs, and then she heard someone laughing and her hair was all ruffled up. We couldn't help but smile: it did look funny, because she normally didn't have a hair out of place.

From then on she wouldn't go for her breaks upstairs unless someone else was with her.

It was Christmas Eve and I was looking forward to going out with friends from work to celebrate. We had arranged to go to a pub in town, it was Avril's favourite local. We always had a laugh when we got together, but being Christmas we felt we were bound to have a great time.

I had bought a short, sexy black dress in the hope that it would make me seem older than sixteen so I could get served at the bar.

I was almost ready to go out, when Michael appeared in front of me and said, "Don't go."

"What do you mean Michael?" I asked, but then I heard my friends coming down the road and I put the finishing touches to my make-up. They were already laughing hysterically so I just knew it was going to be the best night.

We set off to the pub. There was a large crowd already in there when we arrived. We had not realised there was a duo playing that night, but we did manage, after a struggle, to get a table at the back of the pub.

We all had Cinzano and lemonade, their drink of the month. I did not know what to expect as I had only ever tried a little cider when I was thirteen. It was OK and went down easily.

I noticed a bloke sitting opposite us who kept looking over at me.

"Be careful," Michael said.

"What are you on about Michael, what's wrong?" I said in my head.

Michael said nothing more.

I squeezed Avril's arm and said look at that bloke, he keeps looking at me, isn't he cute. She looked over at him, and having already downed two drinks in a matter of minutes, stood up and headed toward him. I felt a bit awkward, but after she spoke to him he came straight over to our table and sat next to me. When I had chance to turn back to Avril I said, "What did you say to him?"

"I just told him you fancied him that's all," she said. I could have died on the spot. I felt my face flush and my stomach drop. I was so embarrassed.

He told me his name was Richard and he lived at the other side of town to me. He was very easy to talk to, even over the loud music. He told me he loved playing guitar and that was part of the reason he came with his mates that night.

After a few more drinks he said he would go and ask if he could do a number with the duo. I think he was just trying to impress me. However he got up and sang with them and I thought he was excellent. That was it, I was hooked – I had never felt this way about anyone before. At the end of the evening he wrote his telephone number down for me and asked me to phone him the next day, which was Christmas Day.

I was in two minds whether or not to ring; after all it was Christmas Day, we had both been the worse for wear with drinking, and maybe he had already forgotten me.

"Think carefully Susan, please think," Michael kept coming into my thoughts, but I was not sure if it was my own fear of rejection, or a warning from him.

However, I did pluck up courage and phoned Richard Christmas afternoon and he was very pleased to hear from me. He was just as charming on the phone as he had been the night before.

If only I had realised then what that phone call had meant for my future, I would never have called him.

We met a few days later at the bus station café. He bought me a cup of tea and we talked for ages. I told him I worked full time and enjoyed it. I told him about my friends, about the school I had attended and just a little about my family. I didn't want to tell him my mum had left us – not yet anyway.

He also told me lots about himself. At one point he confided that he always felt his mum loved his other brothers more than him (something I could relate to). He had had a weekend job at stables just outside of Windsor up until the middle of November, when he had to leave. I asked him why, and he explained that he had been having a sexual relationship with the woman who owned the stables and was his boss. He continued to tell me the story of what happened. His mum knew about the affair, and disapproved because his boss was the same age as her. Richard told me he had been infatuated by her and thought he really loved her. One Saturday morning in early November he walked in on her having sex with another stable hand. He was devastated – she had told him he was a special boy. He told me he went straight home and got a bottle of something from his dad's drinks cabinet and a couple of bottle of pills from his mum's bedside drawer and took the lot.

His mum found him semi-conscious and hanging off his bed. She phoned an ambulance and he had his stomach pumped in the Accident and Emergency Department. He was allowed home a couple of hours later under his mum's supervision.

We went for a walk round a park and continued talking. I felt so sorry for him and realised how vulnerable he must be at the moment. It made me feel more in love with him; he was pouring out his heart to me, wanting, needing me to listen and understand him. I also realised that other people have hard times in their lives and that I really couldn't complain, after all I had never once even contemplated suicide. He needed me and I felt wanted.

We continued to date and after only six weeks Richard asked me to marry him. I told him I really did love him but it was far too soon for that. He sulked and was in a bad mood for weeks afterwards. I was young and was in love with him. His mood upset me and I kept trying to make things alright again.

"Think Susan," Michael said.

"Think what Michael?" I asked.

Right from the beginning Richard needed constant reassurance that he looked good, and asked things like, "Why did I like him? Was I faithful and would we stay together?" He was jealous of everyone, even my female friends and hated me going out with them. I hardly saw them anymore outside work. I could not see anything wrong in it originally. It seemed flattering that he wanted me all to himself.

On the rare occasion I did go out with my friends, he would sit outside my house to monitor what time I got back in. He said it was to make sure I was home safely.

I soon learned the truth, because every time I went out with friends we would have a massive argument the next day. He told me that if I did not go out with my friends he would not get jealous and the arguments would not happen – in effect blaming me. As time went on it seemed easier to go along with what he wanted, and I went out with friends less and less.

Although Richard was often verbally aggressive towards me, a Saturday in June 1976 was the first time he was physically abusive.

I caught a bus to go to meet him down town. One of my brother's friends, Karl, got on the bus and sat next to me. I had known Karl for years; he was a nice boy and a good friend of Joe's. When I stood up on the bus and said goodbye to Karl, Richard must have seen me because when I got off he rushed over to me, his face full of hatred.

"Who the hell was that?" he almost spat at me.

I tried to explain, but he was shouting over me and I started to cry. I could not see because of the tears running down my cheeks. I turned around and walked away from him; I just wanted to go home. The next thing I knew I was pushed very hard from behind. I went flying forward and fell heavily to the ground. My hands and knees were hurting and I was extremely upset. I shouted at him to get lost!

Suddenly, his whole manner changed and he helped me up off the ground. He kept saying how sorry he was and how much he loved me. It was just that he loved me so much he could not bear to see me with another man, and thought I was having an affair. He explained that he could not help being suspicious after what his ex-girlfriend had done.

My knees and hands were bleeding and felt very sore, my tights were ruined and I just wanted to get back home. He kept apologising all the way, and I fell for his promises that he would never do it again. He even managed to make me feel sorry for him!

Michael kept coming into my thoughts saying, "Susan, please think about this relationship, you don't deserve to be treated this way."

Still I continued to go out with Richard – I believed his lies.

It was the hottest summer for years. I went to lunch with Avril in the staff room and we were talking and I had that feeling again: the Dreads. I started to talk about her dad, and asked how long her parents had been together. I really felt the need to tell her to get her dad to go to the doctor. She said he was fine.

I said, "Well when he says he's not well, get him to go." She said she would try, but he did not like the medical profession. She asked me a few questions about my family and we went back to work.

I kept getting the feeling that something wasn't right with Avril's dad over the next couple of days, but I didn't know why. Two days later Avril didn't show for work, which was completely out of character for her. An hour or two into the working day Sandy received a telephone call from Avril's mum to say that Avril's dad had died in the night so Avril wouldn't be coming to work for a while. I felt bad because of our conversation a couple of days earlier.

Michael suddenly appeared and I asked him why Spirit hadn't stressed to me the importance of what I was getting from them. The answer I got was that it was to reassure Avril that there is life after death, so that she could cope with the death of her father.

I also learnt that day that we cannot change the outcome of the things that are meant to be. Everyone's life is mapped out even before they are born.

All of us at the boutique chipped in and sent her some flowers.